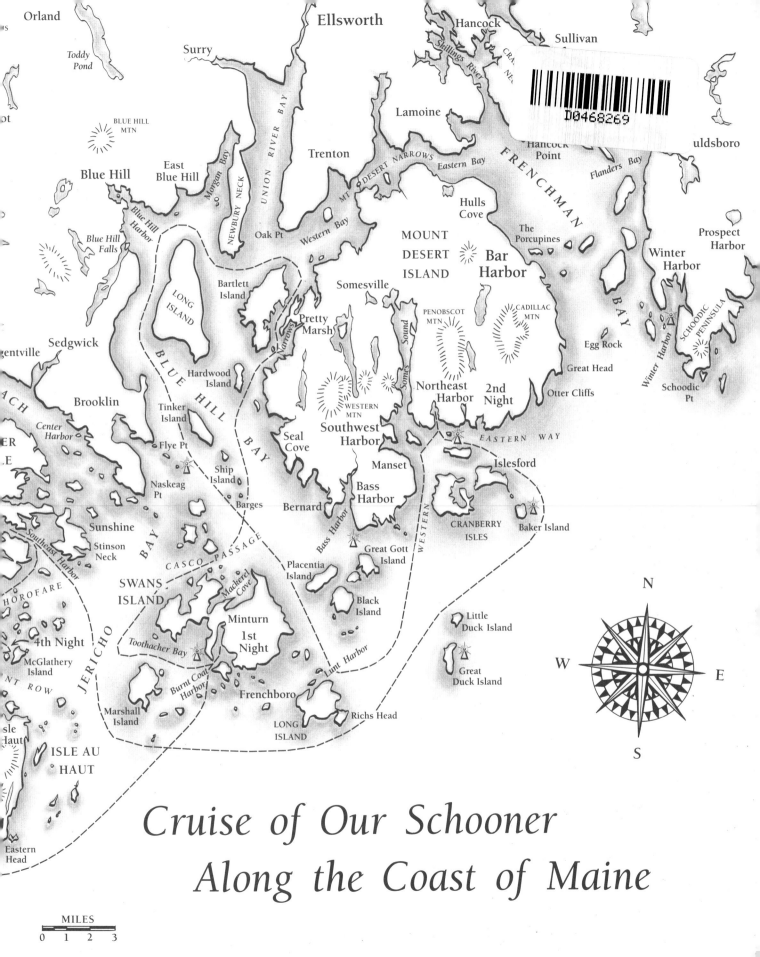

Cruise of Our Schooner
Along the Coast of Maine

A Passage in Time

A Passage in Time

Along the Coast of Maine
by Schooner

Peter H. Spectre

Photographs by Benjamin Mendlowitz

W. W. NORTON & COMPANY
NEW YORK · LONDON

Portions of this book, in significantly different form, have appeared in
WoodenBoat, Down East, Le Chasse Marée, and *Yankee* magazines.

The text of this book is composed in Bauer Bodoni
with the display set in Bodoni bold.
Book design by Sherry Streeter
Printed in Hong Kong

First Edition

Library of Congress Cataloging-in-Publication Data
Spectre, Peter H.
    A passage in time : along the coast of Maine by schooner / Peter
H. Spectre : photographs by Benjamin Mendlowitz.
        p.   cm.
    ISBN 0-393-02997-2 : $45.00
    1. Maine—description and travel—Anecdotes. 2. Schooners—Maine–
History—Anecdotes. 3. Maine—Description and travel—1981—
Views. I. Mendlowitz, Benjamin. II. Title.
F19.6.S64   1991
387.2'24'09741—dc20   44976   12/97   91-10459
                                                                CIP

ISBN 0-393-02997-2
W.W. Norton & Company, Inc., 500 Fifth Avenue, New York, N.Y.
W.W. Norton & Company Ltd., 10 Coptic Street, London WC1A IPU

1 2 3 4 5 6 7 8 9 0

Contents

To Deborah and Eileen

Acknowledgments

The author and photographer would like to thank the following for their assistance:

Captain James Sharp of the schooner *Adventure*; Captains Douglas and Linda Lee of the schooner *Heritage*; Captains Ken and Ellen Barnes of the schooner *Stephen Taber*; Captain John Foss of the schooner *American Eagle*; and Captain Stephen Cobb of the schooner *Mary Day*; Meg Maiden and Roberta Greany of Designwrights; and all the members of the Maine Windjammer Association.

Jonathan Wilson of *WoodenBoat* magazine; Joseph Gribbins of *Nautical Quarterly*; Patience Wales of *Sail* magazine; Dale Kuhnert and Davis Thomas of *Down East* magazine; John Pierce of *Yankee* magazine; and Bernard and Michele Cadoret of *Le Chasse Marée* magazine.

Our special thanks go to those who helped in the production of this book: Llewellyn Howland III of Howland & Co.; James Mairs and Cecil Lyon of W.W. Norton; Kathleen Brandes of Wordsworth Editorial Services; Sherry Streeter of Streeter Design; and Claire Cramer of Mendlowitz Photography.

Our extra-special thanks go to those who encouraged us while we worked on this project: Deborah Brewster, Will and Eachan Holloway, and Samuel and Hannah Mendlowitz; and Eileen, Maureen, Nathan, and Emily Spectre.

Benjamin Mendlowitz
Brooklin, Maine

Peter H. Spectre
Camden, Maine

About the Photographer

I first met Benjamin Mendlowitz in the late 1970s, when he was assigned by *WoodenBoat* magazine to illustrate an article I had written about antique marine engines. My most recent previous experience with a photographer had been on another article for another magazine. That fellow, who was well known and well respected in the trade, took several hundred exposures to produce about five publishable prints. It seemed terribly wasteful to me, and I told him so. It was as if I had written five hundred sentences and then searched through the pile, pulled together a handful to make a short paragraph, and threw away the rest.

The photographer assured me that his routine was typical in the professional photography business. It was easier to grind film through the camera and hope for the best than it was to wait for a long, long time for the right moment to trip the shutter. The law of averages virtually guaranteed that out of five hundred shots, one percent of them *had* to be good.

So it was therefore a refreshing change of pace to work with Benjamin Mendlowitz, who approached the antique-engine assignment with a level of care and appreciation that went far beyond what I had come to expect. Yet he did this without losing the enthusiasm necessary to produce first-rate results. Mendlowitz was, above all, unhurried. He studied each situation carefully, looking for the right light, the right angle, the right feeling that would evoke the essence of the machinery being photographed—for that is what it was, machinery, old engines with brass carburetors and polished steel connecting rods and enameled cylinder heads. He may not have exposed much film that day, but the shots he took revealed those engines in splendid fashion: not only what they were, but also what they were about. In photography, you can't ask for much more than that.

In the late 1970s, Benjamin Mendlowitz was just getting started in marine photography. He had grown up in New York City, then attended Brandeis University in Boston, where he studied physics primarily and film secondarily. He traveled in Europe for a while, and afterward came back to Massachusetts, where he obtained a job with a small company that produced film strips and training films for doctors and hospitals. Several years later, he went out on his own, taking assignments where he could get them. In his travels he met Jonathan Wilson, who had founded *WoodenBoat* magazine in Maine a few years earlier.

Wilson recognized in Mendlowitz a photographer who may have been in the early stages of developing his talent but who was nevertheless able to reveal the singular beauty of wooden boats. As a boy, Mendlowitz spent many summers on the New Jersey shore, where he loved to hang around the boatyards and came to appreciate classically designed and built boats. As a freelance photographer, he had taken photographs of some of the

International One-Design sailing class, and even though he was not specializing in marine photography at the time, his work rivaled that of photographers who were. Think of what he could do if he actually studied the field!

Which is what he went on to do. With the encouragement of Wilson and his associate Maynard Bray of *WoodenBoat* magazine, Mendlowitz spent more and more time photographing classic boats, the traditional watercraft that at the time seemed to be an endangered species. His work was featured extensively in the pages of *WoodenBoat*—so much so that many readers thought he was the staff photographer, even though he was not an employee. As time passed, Mendlowitz saw his photographs published in other nautical magazines as well, such as *Sail* and *Nautical Quarterly*. The latter was noted for the excellence of its reproduction, which made good photographs look great and great ones, like Mendlowitz's, look extraordinary. And then, in 1983, he published the *Calendar of Wooden Boats*, the first of an annual edition of his best photographs—a publication that is now as classic as the boats it features.

Marine photography has a long tradition, as long as the history of photography itself. Each era has produced its stars—among them the successive generations of Bekens of Cowes and the Gibsons of the Scilly Isles; W.B. Jackson of Massachusetts; Edwin Levick of New York; and the Rosenfelds, father and son, also of New York. Their styles may have been different, but all these photographers shared a common trait: They understood boats. Not just by being able to tell one boat type from another—a sloop from a cutter or a schooner from a ketch. Rather, they understood the lines of boats, the shapes of boats, the way boats moved in a seaway. Whether this understanding was intuitive or acquired from study, I do not know. But I do know that such an appreciation allowed them to elevate their work from taking pictures of boats to creating images of boats as fine art.

All of those photographers in a general sense confined their work to what they considered to be beautiful boats, and Benjamin Mendlowitz carries on in that tradition. Not only is Mendlowitz selective in the shots he takes—the lighting, the focus, the angle, the mood—he also is selective about the boats he chooses to photograph. His subjects tend to be the old classics or modern craft influenced by traditional design. A photograph by Benjamin Mendlowitz is more than the result of a click of the camera. It is more than a pretty picture, attractively presented. It is more than depth of field and sharp focus and color fidelity and all of the rest of photography's mechanics and techniques. It is, simply stated, the result of the photographer's ability to convey to the viewer that he not only has seen the boat through the lens of his camera, but also has understood what he has seen.

—Peter H. Spectre

A Passage in Time

1 *One Vast Neighborhood*

*The era of [commercial] sail has gone, giving place to science and the
quickened pulse of the present, but to many who saw and knew them,
the passing of these old vessels and the resourceful men who sailed
them is tinged with sadness. In another decade or so, there will be no
memory to bring back the cough of the donkey engine, the rattle of
anchor chain, and the thundering of wind-filled canvas; none to
remember the leaning spars and the bellying topsails against the
blue sky or the looming of ghostly hulls through the fog.*

     —John F. Leavitt, *Wake of the Coasters, 1970*

Fog bisected the island. At one end, facing the mainland, the sun shone brightly in a
cloudless, deep-blue sky. At the other, facing the bay, the air was thick with moisture.
Standing by one tree in the dense spruce forest, I could barely see the next. Fine droplets
of water ran down the spruce needles, coalesced, and fell to the ground. Scarcely a breeze
stirred the branches.

I had rowed across the harbor, stepping ashore on the sunny side of the little island,
pulling my skiff high up the shingled shore for protection against the rising tide. I tied the
painter to an ancient iron stake that years ago had been driven into the rock by an
unknown soulmate, climbed the bank, and crossed the island on a wide path that had been
cut through the woods by the crew of coastguardsmen who once manned the lighthouse
out on the point. This path and the lighthouse itself, invisible in the fog, were their
monuments. A white sign with dark blue lettering—All Persons Are Warned Not to Injure
or Disturb any Property of the U.S. Coast Guard—was their epitaph. One second I was
in the sun, filled with hope; the next I was in the gloom of the fog.

The keeper's house was empty, the windows boarded up with sheets of cardboard
painted gray. The steps that led to the kitchen door, rotting unevenly, had pulled away
from the building and were slowly moldering into the ground. Every minute or so the big
foghorn, mounted on a granite plinth, groaned through the fog. It was an automaton;
nobody was at the switch. I was alone on the island with a bundle of wires and transistors
and fog-sensing devices.

Compared to the bustle of the town at the head of the harbor, only half a mile or so away
as the gull flies, it was a scene of incredible loneliness and desolation. I sat down in a small
depression in the ledge that sloped away from the lighthouse into the bay and poured a

**"The sounds came
from out in the
bay, somewhere
off to the right."**

mug of steaming coffee from the thermos I carried in my knapsack. This is better, I thought to myself. But it wasn't. I thought about leaving.

Then the sounds came from out in the bay, somewhere off to the right. A clattering of pans, the rattling of chain, the weak bleat of a horn, muttering voices of several people who sounded as if they were whispering to each other at the bottom of a deep well, then a bellow of command.

"We're going to jibe! Mate? Grab that sheet!"

Another loud voice: "Let her rip!"

"You! On the cabinhouse. Watch your head!"

There was the sound of a heavy block sliding quickly along an iron traveler, and a whacking snap as it came up short, and squeaking sheaves as a sheet was adjusted, and then a moment of silence. I strained to see through the murk. Nothing. Only the gently increasing swish of a large hull pushing water aside.

"Katy? Can you see the island?"

"Not yet."

"The channel buoy?"

"No...wait...." A pause. "I can see something to port...a lighthouse...a ledge...trees.... Someone is standing on the ledge...."

Someone is standing on the ledge. That's me, I thought. And then I saw it—a big coasting schooner sliding along as if in a dream. It didn't jump out of the fog as much as gradually emerge from behind a translucent curtain. First there was impenetrable gray, and then gray with a darkish center, and then a hardening of the center, and then indistinct bulk, and then—bang—an instant revelation: a two-masted wooden schooner, the foresail wung out to starboard, the mainsail out to port. The vessel was so close to shore that I felt as if I could reach out and grab the end of the main boom, swing myself onto it, walk inboard along its length, and drop onto the deck.

It was an optical illusion, of course, and a fantasy—a fantasy! Was it a fantasy? Weren't the coasting schooners as dead as the steamer service to Boston? Was this wishful thinking?

The lookout at the base of the bowsprit, a woman, smiled across as calmly as if we were passing on a narrow sidewalk. The cook poked his head out of the main companionway hatch, glanced around, shrugged his shoulders, and disappeared below. The skipper, at the wheel, said something to a woman sitting on the cabinhouse and pointed at me.

"Right on the nose," he yelled with a grin. A few feet farther in and he would have struck the ledge. A few feet farther out and he would have missed the harbor entrance.

"You'll be out of it in a minute or two," I yelled back, my voice echoing off the side of the broad wooden hull. "The harbor is clear."

And then the schooner was gone, receding into the fog as quickly as it had emerged. The year was 1980, just about the time when John F. Leavitt, schoonerman and historian, expected all memories of the Maine coasting schooners to have disappeared. His prediction had been wrong.

"And then I saw it—a big coasting schooner sliding along as if in a dream."

Penobscot Bay lies midway along the coast of Maine. Though people to the westward—which is to say, residents of Boston and the rest of New England—regard all of the Maine coast as the mythical land of "Down East," Mainers define the western edge of that territory as the eastern edge of Penobscot Bay. All places east of the bay are "to the east'ard" and therefore "down east." All those west of it are "to the west'ard." The bay is the center of things, the heart of the coast of Maine—"one vast neighborhood," as John Leavitt wrote in a fit of nostalgia in *Wake of the Coasters*, the most entertainingly accessible memory of the last years of cargo-carrying commercial sail in Maine.

Penobscot Bay is significant in size as New England bays go. Though not nearly as large as Cape Cod Bay, it is nevertheless larger than Buzzards and Narragansett and makes its Maine competitors—Casco, Muscongus, Blue Hill, and even Passamaquoddy, to name but a few—look puny by comparison. Twenty miles wide at the mouth, Isle au Haut to Whitehead, and twenty-eight miles long (twenty-four miles longer if you include the stretch from Fort Point to Bangor, the navigable part of the Penobscot River, which drains into the northern neck of the bay), it is magnificent by anyone's standards. From the land, however—the low land—from Route 1, which runs along most of the bay's western shore, and from the back roads of the eastern side, it doesn't look that large. Too many headlands and islands obstruct the view.

To appreciate the size and sweep of Penobscot Bay from the land, you have to climb one of the many mountains along its edges, just as the young poet Edna St. Vincent Millay did years ago on the western shore:

> *All I could see from where I stood*
> *Was three long mountains and a wood;*
> *I turned and looked the other way,*
> *And saw three islands in a bay.*
> *So with my eyes I traced the line*
> *Of the horizon, thin and fine,*
> *Straight around till I was come*
> *Back to where I'd started from....*

It's best to study the layout of Penobscot Bay on one of those late fall days when a light breeze is blowing diagonally across the bay from the northwest, down out of Canada and across the western mountains, pushing the last drop of warm-weather moisture out into the Atlantic. There will be no distortions in the atmosphere, no haziness on the horizon to fuzz up the edges of the islands or obscure the peak of Cadillac on Mount Desert, no fog sitting like a glob of oozing muck over the Fox Islands. It will be too early for winter sea smoke, but not so late as to bring cold that might keep you from lingering over the view. The dominant colors will be the ice blue of the sky, the deep purple of the bay, the dark green of the islands, the grays and tans of the rocky shore, and the flaming reds and yellows and oranges of the hardwood forests climbing the sides of the hills and mountains.

Mount Battie, Mount Megunticook, or Bald Rock on the western shore. Waldo, halfway up the river toward Bangor. Caterpillar, on the eastern side, or Isle au Haut (High Island) down to the southeast, a wild and beautiful place around which spreads the panorama of Maine's mid-coast: the islands of Monhegan and Matinicus, Vinalhaven and North Haven, Islesboro, Deer, and Metinic, and, farther down east, Mount Desert and Swans; the principal towns of Rockland and Camden, Rockport, Belfast, Searsport, Bucksport, Castine, and Stonington; the East Bay and the West Bay, and, along an arc that extends from the northeast point of the compass around to the southwest, the wild yet beckoning Gulf of Maine and the Atlantic Ocean.

But, as any sailor will tell you, the best way to get a feel for the bay is not from the peak of a mountain but from the deck of a boat or a ship. Meet the bay from seaward. Sail in from the Atlantic, making your first landfall the lighthouse on Matinicus Rock. Sail southwestward from the Bay of Fundy, turning the corner at Roaring Bull Ledge off Isle au Haut. Cruise down from Boston on an end-of-summer southwesterly; sail downwind inside Monhegan and Matinicus, through the Muscle Ridge or the more open Two Bush Channel, into West Penobscot Bay, the mainland to port, the spruce-covered islands to starboard, the choices for a snug anchorage out of the wind and the weather, infinite.

If you come in on a cruising boat, you will think you have discovered the last unspoiled stretch of the coast this side of the Canadian maritime provinces. If you come in on a commercial vessel—a tanker, a freighter, a fishing boat—and you have some historical sensitivity, you will know why, during the maritime heyday of Maine in the last decades of the last century, hundreds of shipmasters, including almost a hundred in Searsport alone, when they weren't roaming the oceans of the world in clippers, Down Easters, and big coal and lumber schooners, called Penobscot Bay their home.

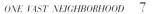

Penobscot Bay—the entire coast of Maine, for that matter—once was crowded with sailing vessels. Coastal cargo carriers, passenger packets, fishing craft, naval vessels, deepwater traders, so many at any one time that the waters were white with sails. The bay was like a huge highway of sail, with the rivers and creeks that fed into it the secondary roads. One town was connected to the next, one area of the bay to another, by a watery thoroughfare that was as familiar to the sailors who manned the vessels as the Maine Turnpike is to today's travelers. To grasp the complexity of the system, imagine a map of today's overland roads around Penobscot Bay and overlay it on the bay and its tributaries.

Sail was everywhere. To grasp the quantity, consider that in 1860 at the Penobscot River port of Bangor—which today rarely sees motor vessels—never mind sail, there were more than 3,000 arrivals during a navigation season that lasted not much longer than six months. On the fourteenth of July in that year, sixty sailing vessels made the port on an incoming tide in the space of two hours. Every one of those vessels passed through Penobscot Bay.

Consider the keeper of the lighthouse at Owls Head, a high headland that marks the end of the approaches to West Penobscot Bay and the lower corner of the outside channel

Owls Head, the
southern corner of
Rockland Harbor on
the western shore of
Penobscot Bay. The
Camden Hills are on
the horizon to the
north. The keeper of
the Owls Head Light
counted 16,000
schooners passing this
point in the year 1876,
which would average
out to almost two
schooners an hour,
day and night.

Pumpkin Island, one of hundreds of little islands in the Penobscot Bay region. Once maintained by the Coast Guard as an aid to navigation, the lighthouse, situated just inside Eggemoggin Reach, is now a private residence.

to Rockland Harbor. In 1876, the keeper counted more than 16,000 schooners from his lookout. Just schooners. That figure does not include steamers or sailing vessels with other rigs—sloops, brigs, brigantines, barques, etc.—which no doubt also represented a significant amount.

The keeper's 1876 count is an oft-quoted statistic, though it may seem a trifle unrealistic from today's perspective. After all, 16,000 amounts to almost two schooners an hour, night and day, fair weather and foul, summer and winter. Throw in the other types of ships and boats and you must be talking about a vessel passing the light about every ten or fifteen minutes, which is possible but not likely. What is more likely is that the lighthouse keeper stepped outside once an hour and counted the vessels in view. If the same vessels from the previous hour were still there—becalmed, for example—then each would be counted again as if it were a different vessel.

But that's not the point. There were so many sailing vessels on Penobscot Bay in the latter part of the nineteenth century that it was difficult to get an accurate count. So to be safe, halve the lightkeeper's number. What the hell, halve it again. That would be 4,000 schooners in one year—almost a dozen every day, all year round! Never mind the sailing vessels of other rigs.

By comparison, the Penobscot Bay of our time is a very quiet place indeed. Even during the height of summer in the most ideal sailing conditions, you could climb the steps to Owls Head Light or walk to the end of the Rockland breakwater or stand on the shore of the Fox Islands Thorofare and count the sailing vessels—include the modern pleasure craft to inflate the figure if you wish—and the number will look puny in comparison to the same day a century ago. But, contrary to the views of many who claim to have seen the death of commercial sail on the coast of Maine, you will find in your number several commercial sailing vessels—coasters that pay their way and that of their owners and crews by earning real money—not a lot, but enough to keep alive a tradition that otherwise would be found only in the pages of books and the halls of museums.

In the north end of Rockland, the largest town on Penobscot Bay and until recent years a major fishing port, there's a grocery store called Jordan's Market. It's an unpretentious establishment occupying the Crockett Block, a onetime fine old building that was rehabbed in the early 1980s to a style thought to be tacky in the 1950s—if you know what I mean. It's a schizophrenic store, a cross between a Depression-era catchall and a 7-Eleven with a fish market grafted onto the back. They carry the Portland and Boston papers, beer by the bottle, a mixed bag of canned goods, slack-salted cod, haddock and the occasional halibut, and, in season, smoked bloaters. There's nothing remarkable about the place except for a bronze plaque screwed to the outside wall next to the side door. The inscription reads:

Fast Clipper Ship "Red Jacket"
Still Holds World Speed Record
For Sailing in Voyage from
Sandy Hook to Liverpool
In January, 1854, 13 Days, One Hour
Launched at George Thomas's Ship
Yard in Rear of Crockett Block
November 2, 1853 at 11 A.M.
          Asa Eldridge, Master

It's difficult to imagine. Right here on this spot, right here where you can buy a 24-inch Slim Jim, a six-pack of Budweiser, and the latest edition of the *National Enquirer*; right next to a shop where they fix lawn mowers; right on the curb of Route 1—the Canadian border to the tip of Florida, more used-car lots and fast-food restaurants than any highway in the country, perhaps the world—George Thomas and his crew of shipwrights built the clipper *Red Jacket*, for a time the most famous ship in the Western world, 251 feet long, 44 feet beam, 2,306 tons.

✦

November 2, 1853. It was quite a morning. Thousands were on hand for the launching, more people than present-day Rockland sees for its annual Lobster Festival. There were celebrants from as far away as New York and Philadelphia—this in a time when it would have taken an event of incredible importance for people to brave traveling halfway down the Maine coast so late in the year. There were speeches and band playing and ceremonies and tours of the ship. The after cabin was a stunning affair finished out with select rosewood, mahogany, zebrawood, black walnut, and satinwood and decorated with gilded accents. The figurehead, surrounded with gilt scrollwork, was "Red Jacket" himself—Sagoyewatha, chief of the Senecas, wearing his trademark scarlet tunic given by the British as a gesture of friendship.

The *Red Jacket* was by no means the only ship built in Rockland, and George Thomas was not the only master builder to ply his trade there. From the town's founding in 1767, hundreds of ships and thousands of boats were built in scores of shipyards and boatshops that at various times—especially during the mid- to late nineteenth century—lined the waterfront from just above Jordan's Market in the north end to Head of the Bay in the south.

But that was then and this is now. The closest thing to the *Red Jacket* in today's Rockland is a restaurant-and-bar by that name down by the Sears store and a model of the vessel in the Farnsworth Museum just off Main Street. Oh, yes, and a bunch of passenger schooners berthed at the North End Shipyard wharf, down the little road between Jordan's Market and the shop next door—the one that claims to be the second-largest dealer in used hubcaps in the state of Maine. These schooners may be a tad rustic when compared to the *Red Jacket* and tiny in comparison to the big four-, five-, and six-masted coal and lumber schooners of the turn of the century, but they nevertheless are a link in an unbroken chain that stretches back to the earliest sailing vessels on the coast of Maine.

"Oh, yes, and a bunch of
passenger schooners berthed
at the North End Shipyard
wharf, down the little road
between Jordan's Market
and the shop next door."

II *A Smoky Sou'wester*

He was jovial, kind hearted, and a bit of a philosopher. In one phrase he summarized the call of the sea. When I asked him if he liked the life afloat he replied, "No, I hate it. But I can't keep away from it. I tell you what it is, mister. You give me the choice of my wife or the vessel, I take the vessel."
—Frederick Sturgis Laurence on Captain William R. Kreger
of the four-masted schooner *Sarah C. Ropes*

We cast off about eleven o'clock Monday morning, the last passenger schooner to clear the North End Shipyard wharf. The skipper had spent half the morning at the bank, arguing with the officers about a loan to carry him through the coming winter, when he planned to join another schoonerman in rebuilding an old vessel. "They're all jugheads," he muttered to himself as he dragged his charts out of their cases and spread them flat on the roof of the after cabinhouse, just forward of the wheel. He weighted down the corners with little leather pouches filled with lead shot, like beanbags.

The passengers, most of whom had arrived the previous afternoon and evening, amused themselves during the seemingly interminable wait by helping the mate and galley hand make baggywrinkle—odd pieces of frayed rope used to pad the rigging so it won't wear holes in the sails—or hanging around in the galley, drinking coffee and pestering the cook. I spent the time exploring the schooner and studying the other vessels as they got underway.

We were in the center of the largest group of working schooners alongside any single wharf on the coast of Maine, nestled together and rising and falling like a flock of ducks in the gentle swell of Rockland Harbor. The *J. & E. Riggin*, a former oyster dredger built in 1927; the *Isaac H. Evans*, another oyster boat, 1886; the *Lewis R. French*, a fishing schooner and freight carrier, 1871; the *American Eagle*, a fishing schooner, 1930; and the *Heritage*, a coasting schooner launched in 1983. Over by the state ferry terminal was the *Stephen Taber*, a brick schooner, 1871. Three other passenger schooners were across the harbor by the town landing: the *Nathaniel Bowditch*, a former yacht and fishing dragger built in 1922, the *Summertime*, a double-ended pinky schooner launched especially for the passenger trade in 1986, and the three-masted schooner *Domino Effect*.

There may not have been as many working sailing vessels in Rockland Harbor as there had been when the lime industry was in full swing, when wood-boats by the hundreds were hauling in cordwood to fire the kilns and a vast fleet of schooners was carrying away casks

The *Nathaniel Bowditch*, a former yacht and fishing dragger, sets out for a week along the coast —"the destination nowhere in particular, the goal an opportunity to escape whatever must be escaped and live a nineteenth-century life in the twentieth century."

of lime for Boston and New York, but today, when a salty craft is thought to be a boat built of polyester resin and glass strands shoveled into a mold, nine vessels authentically fitted out in the old style and setting sail at once are nothing to sneeze at.

A similar scene was taking place up the bay in Camden, where four wooden schooners (*Mary Day*, 1962; *Roseway*, 1925; *Mercantile*, 1916; *Grace Bailey*, 1882; *Mistress*, 1960) and a steel ketch (*Angelique*, 1980) were getting underway, and in Rockport, where the pilot schooner *Timberwind*, 1931, had slipped her lines and was beating out of the harbor.

Our schooner wasn't the largest of the fleet (the *Domino Effect* held that distinction), but she was one of the prettiest. She was 72 feet long, not including the bowsprit, and 21 feet wide, and could carry 3,500 square feet of canvas on her two-masted rig. She had white topsides accented with a dark-gray sheerstrake (the topmost plank on the hull), white cabinhouse sides, buff on all the horizontal surfaces such as the roofs of the houses, oiled decks and spars, a black iron steering wheel, and a white bowsprit enlivened with a bronze star on the flat of the end. Other decorations included maroon stars incised, top and bottom, on the two water casks on either side of the mainmast, a carved nameboard on the stern featuring an encircling rope, gilded, and trailboards that followed the sweep of the bow up to the stem and were embellished with relief carvings of ivy, also gilded, and a pair of red roses. Underway, she carried a long, forest-green streamer at the head of the maintopmast.

A coastal packet built near the end of the last century, our schooner, until World War II, carried general cargo along the Maine coast—lumber, coal, salt, case goods, the type of loads now hauled over highways by tractor-trailer trucks. At the beginning of the war she was laid up, and, like so many of the coasting schooners that joined her, never returned to her original trade. Rather, like most of the schooners in the Maine wind-jammer fleet, she was converted to passenger-carrying and now sails out of Rockland on week-long cruises, Monday through Saturday, mid-June to late September, the destination nowhere in particular, the goal an opportunity for her paying passengers to escape whatever must be escaped and live a nineteenth-century life in the twentieth century.

The accommodations were—how can I put this delicately?—a little tight. What had once been the hold—the area between the after cabin and the forecastle, between the two masts—was partitioned into what the advertising brochure euphemistically termed "staterooms." There were six of these doubles and quadruples, with bunks for eighteen people. Very friendly people. If you should ever find yourself with an enemy on a windjammer, you can be sure that (a) you will, of necessity, become friends, or (b) you will flip a coin to determine who will sleep up on deck in the lee of the longboat. There were two "staterooms" off the after cabin; the rest of the below-decks space was given over to the crew's accommodations (even more spartan than those of the passengers, if that could be possible) and the galley. The bunks were narrow and the headroom was non-existent if you were more than six feet tall; the turning-around space was just about right for a contortionist. Each passenger got two sheets and a pillowcase, two woolen blankets, and a bath towel.

Narrow bunks, adventurous headroom, the coziness of a cabin on a sailing vessel. Schooner accommodations vary from spartan, with wash basins issued to each person, to relatively comfortable, with running water—perhaps hot, perhaps not.

The *Roseway*

There was running fresh water in the galley for the convenience of the dishwasher—who plied her trade in a corner between the wood-burning stove and boxes of provisions—but nowhere else on the vessel. Each passenger was issued a tin cup and a tin washbasin. Water was obtained from the casks on deck, with long-handled dippers. Brushing one's teeth before bed was an adventure; likewise, shaving in the morning. Hot water was not totally unavailable, but getting a jar full of it meant competing for space on top of the galley stove with the cook, the dishwasher, and the coffee addicts, all of whom claimed first priority. The toilets—"heads" in nautical parlance—didn't flush in the conventional sense; instead, they were operated with a hand pump.

There were no television, no radio other than the skipper's (which he guarded as closely as his navigational tools), no wall-to-wall carpeting, no telephone, and no light bulbs larger than 15 watts. On the other hand, for entertainment there was a tiny pump organ and a collection of sheet music in the after cabin—which, like the galley, was illuminated with ornate brass kerosene lanterns—and a small shelf with several books belonging to the skipper. *Dutton's Navigation and Piloting*, the *American Practical Navigator*, *Sailing Days on the Penobscot*, *Islands of the Mid-Maine Coast*, *The History of American Sailing Ships*, that type of thing. For additional entertainment, there was on deck, built into a corner of the forward deckhouse, a minuscule shower stall about the size of a refrigerator box with a single valve that released a spray of cold salt water with less pressure than a drinking-water fountain.

In short, our schooner was much the same as any other sailing vessel of fifty to a hundred years ago, and the experience provided the passengers was ditto. Well, almost but not quite.

In the days of commercial sail, schooner accommodations were a tad ripe, to put it politely. "The crew's quarters," wrote Frederick Sturgis Laurence about the four-master *Sarah C. Ropes*, "...was a black greasy looking apartment with wooden bunks and a stench that would knock you flat. I wondered how many human beings could be content to sleep there...." There were no showers, no running water of any sort on most coasting schooners, and each member of the crew was responsible for his own bedding. He had to bring not only his own blankets, towels, and sheets, but also his own mattress. The latter, made of ticking and straw, was known as a "donkey's breakfast." Each man hand-made his own or bought one for a few cents from a ship's chandler. When the bedbugs became too overwhelming, the mattress was thrown overboard and replaced with a new one.

Nor were there any heads. On the small coasters there was, instead, a wooden bucket with a rope lanyard. The user drew water from over the side, set the bucket down in a quiet corner of the deck, read his mail or studied the Sears catalog, and then emptied the bucket over the side.

The arrangement was more luxurious aboard the large schooners. According to Francis ("Biff") Bowker in *Blue Water Coaster*, a memoir of the author's service before the mast during the dying days of sail on the east coast:

There was a seat attached to the bow on the port side. A lead pipe ran down through the planking for drainage. A pile of old newspapers and magazines served for paper. There was also an oil drum with the head knocked out. This was kept full of salt water, and a paint can was used to dip out water for flushing. This arrangement was all right with the wind on the starboard side or aft of the beam on the port side. It was not so good when the vessel was hard on the port tack and driving into a sea, for the wind and water tended to blow right back up the pipe. Under such conditions a certain amount of skill was necessary for safe operation of this equipment. The first act was to wad up a ball of paper, stuff it into the pipe, and push it down with a stick. When it came time to do the flushing, one would take the stick in one hand and the bucket of water in the other. Then, waiting until the vessel drove her bow into a sea, the stick was jabbed down, the flushing water was thrown in at the same instant, and the operator dove back out of the way as the bows rose and a blast of wind blew back whatever had not found its way into the sea.

The day was sunny and cool, gradually warming as the morning progressed. There were thin clouds in the west and haze building out in the bay, and the weatherman was talking about a front on Wednesday afternoon or night that might or might not be the leading edge of a tropical storm that could very well be upgraded to a hurricane.

"We damn well better be holed up in a tight harbor come Wednesday night," the skipper said, slapping the rim of the steering wheel.

Our schooner, like most other windjammers, didn't have an auxiliary engine. There was, in fact, no power on the vessel other than a bank of batteries and an emergency generator for the lights and the radio, and a small, old-fashioned, one-lung "make-and-break" engine for hoisting the anchor. So we were towed away from the wharf by the yawlboat, a heavily built craft fitted with a big truck engine modified for marine use. Pronounced "yawl-b'ot" by the down-easters, it was so named because the first of its type were ship's boats, ship's yawls, utility boats that were hung in davits over the transom when not in use.

On the Maine coast, the first internal-combustion engines for auxiliary power were fitted in the yawlboats rather than the schooners themselves, because the owners, always thinking of return on investment, resented taking up valuable cargo space with "a goddam hunk of iron." Over the years, the powered yawl became one of the identifying peculiarities of the coasting schooner. It remains in use to this day, partly because it does save space and partly out of a sense of tradition, a condition whose power cannot be underestimated.

Once we were well out into the harbor, the mate in the yawlboat dropped the towline and brought her around to the stern of the schooner, nosing the padded stem of the boat against the schooner's flat stern. Lines were rigged from the bow of the yawlboat up around the after quarters of the schooner. With the yawl thus held and pushing at a steady speed, the mate left her unattended and climbed up to the schooner to help raise the sails. The yawlboat's engine became the schooner's auxiliary power; the skipper controlled both vessels with the steering wheel.

Like their cargo-carrying predecessors—many of which went to sea with only the proverbial "man, boy, and a dog" and a make-and-break hoisting, or "donkey," engine to help with the heavy work—the windjammers are undermanned for their size, relying on the passengers to help handle the sails. Our schooner was no exception. No one was coerced into hauling on the halyards and the sheets, but one look at the huge size of the sails and the diminutive size of the crew—skipper, mate, cook, and galley hand—and everybody on board, lubber or not, *knew* there would be no sailing without a little sweat now and again. The mainsail alone was 1,500 square feet and weighed 500 pounds! So with shouted encouragement from the mate—"Hey, yah, heave!…, Hey, yah, heave!…Now…drop it!"—and bellows of laughter at our clumsiness from the skipper, and a few cases of rope burn, we raised the sails, working from aft, forward. First the main, then the fore, then the forestaysail, then the jib.

Just off the tip of the Rockland breakwater, by the lighthouse, with all sails trimmed and pulling in a southwesterly breeze, the mate jumped down into the yawlboat and shut off the engine. The silence was shocking. We walked around in a daze, smelling the salt air blowing through the pine tar of the rigging and watching a pair of harbor seals at play in a field of lobster-trap buoys to the east of the breakwater. The crew hauled the yawl-boat up into the stern davits with tackles, bow and stern, and the mate yelled, "That's it, folks, we're bound for…"

"Wherever," the skipper added. Perhaps Stonington, he figured. Or maybe North Haven, or Vinalhaven, Isle au Haut, Monhegan. He didn't know and nobody seemed to care. The point was to take a cruise in the wake of the coasters, where the wind took us, not according to schedule.

Swans Island? "Maybe," the skipper said. "All I'm thinking about right now is Wednesday night and a tight little hole protected from a gale in any direction."

"And good holding bottom for the anchor," the mate said.

"For two anchors if we have to," the skipper added.

The mate was a caricature of a sailor. He was in his late twenties or early thirties and wore his long, curly, blond hair in a ponytail. Sometimes when he was painting or working down in the lazarette—a small compartment where he stowed his maintenance gear—he wrapped his head in a red bandanna. He had wire-rim glasses held together in places with tape, forearms like Popeye's, multi-patched dungarees, big calluses on his hands, and a rigger's knife with a blade so sharp it could slice a tomato to one-sixteenth of an inch. He had worked on schooners since he graduated from high school, and he was as competent with a carpenter's saw and a caulking mallet as he was with a marlinspike. He and the skipper had been together so long they finished each other's sentences.

The skipper, a native Mainer, was one of those men of indeterminate age. He could have been thirty-five or forty-five; for that matter, he could have been forty or fifty. He was of medium height, stocky, with black hair, a salt-and-pepper beard, and a lively face. He wore the same clothes all the time: dungarees, dark-blue suspenders with white stripes, red long johns peeking out from under a flannel shirt, sneakers, and, when the air turned

cool, a maroon zip-up sweatshirt with black lettering on the back that said "Head Schoonerman." He smoked cigars and pronounced *schooner* as "skunnah" and slept in his clothes, to the wonder of the passengers. He kept up a constant stream of chatter: he woke up in the morning talking and went to bed at night talking and obviously relished his role. He was part sailor, part actor, part coastal character, part boatbuilder, part storyteller, and part living embodiment of the archetypal coasterman of the past, keeper of the flame. He knew or had heard of everyone in the business, wherever they might be— ship designers, builders, sailors, hangers-on—and he loved his schooner with boundless passion.

"We were out in Gilkey Harbor last week," he said, "and in the evening I rowed ashore

Sweating up the yawl-boat on the schooner *J. & E. Riggin*. The starboard-side gang has the bow up and the crowd on the port side is working on the stern. The padding on the stem of the yawlboat protects the stern of the schooner when she is being pushed.

to see a friend of mine. I looked back at the schooner silhouetted in the sunset behind the Camden Hills and couldn't believe how beautiful she looked. I couldn't believe she was mine."

✪

We were struck with the full force of the rising southwesterly breeze when we passed Owls Head Light. The wind was fighting the ebbing tide, and the resulting steep waves were capped with white foam. Rather than turn down the bay and pound into what the old coastermen used to call "a lump of a head-beat sea," the skipper steered the vessel diagonally across the bay to skirt the White Islands and Hurricane Island, off Vinalhaven's southwestern shore. The rigging on the windward side, taut from the pressure of the wind on the sails, started to thrum. The schooner pitched now and again, throwing spray from her bow. We picked up speed and charged like a thoroughbred for the first sea mark, the buoy at Old Horse Ledge. Some of the passengers, those with a natural affinity for sailing, skylarked around the deck. Others, made nervous by what to them was the strange motion of a windjammer in her element, appeared uneasy; a handful were slightly green around the gills.

"This is sailing weather!" the skipper yelled to nobody in particular. "See the haze on the horizon? A smoky sou'wester."

The southwesterly wind prevails on the Maine coast during the summer months, blowing out of Massachusetts Bay toward the Bay of Fundy. The usual diurnal pattern is light air in the morning, a strong breeze in the afternoon, and calm in the evening. The strongest southwesterly is almost always accompanied by a hazy atmosphere, hence the reference to smoke. Summer will see an occasional westerly, but the more normal deviation from southwest is an easterly or southeasterly wind, usually wet but every once in a while strong, steady, and dry.

Come winter, the northwest wind prevails—a wild, bitter, dry blast out of the depths of Canada. The strongest northwesterly, which usually carries subzero cold in the wake of an intense storm, is nicknamed the "Montreal Express," or some variation thereof. A winter dominated by northwesterlies is extremely cold, and most of the coastal waters consequently become choked with ice, though only rarely does Penobscot Bay itself become icebound. In the winters of 1779–80 and 1875–76, however, the bay froze from Vinalhaven to Bangor; daredevils could walk from Camden to North Haven, Belfast to Castine.

The winter storms, the legendary New England gales, come out of the east and the northeast and bring snow, sleet, freezing rain, ice, you name it. Obviously, the passenger-schooner fleet lies low during the winter months, but in the days of cargo-carrying, many of the coasters kept at it year round.

It was a dangerous business, winter coasting, especially in the later years, when economics virtually ensured that the vessels would be in poor repair and undermanned, and therefore least able to handle the strain. Though it would seem that a schooner sailing along the coast would be secure, in close proximity to harbors of refuge, such was not the case. During any of the common "thicks" of the Maine coast—thick o' fog, thick o' snow, thick o' vapor (sea smoke brought on by extremely cold air lying over warmer water)— the land, unseen by the schoonerman, became more dangerous than the towering seas of the open ocean. There were too many rocks, half-tide ledges, and unpredictable currents.

Little wonder, then, that skippers of winter coasters had the reputation for being cautious—perhaps overly cautious from the point of view of an owner who would be losing money when his schooner hid behind a headland to wait out a northwester or a northeast gale. But can anyone blame the coastermen? They knew all about the limitations of navigating with only a compass, a barometer, and the seats of their pants, even though most of the best skippers were famous for their "nose" for the coast. (Some were even noted for their ability to predict changes in the weather by reference to corns on their feet, sore elbows and knees, and ticks in the corners of their eyes.) The best of them also knew about the consequences of being overconfident. The periodic North Atlantic winter storms provided plenty of evidence, the most famous being the "*Portland* Gale" of November 26–27, 1898, when 456 lives were lost and 141 vessels were wrecked, including the steamer *Portland*, which gave its name to the storm.

But a smoky southwester bears no relationship to the *Portland* Gale or the Montreal Express. We were sailing hard and fast, and the timbers of the schooner were groaning in response to the heaving of the sea and the pressure of the wind, but this was unintimidating summer sailing, not the agony of a hang-on-to-your-hats winter struggle. The wind was steady, not squally, and the skipper's navigational marks—buoys, lighthouses, headlands, and prominent islands—were visible a long way off.

The galley hand came staggering on deck with an armload of dishes and covered bowls and eating utensils, followed by the cook carrying a steaming caldron of fish chowder. It was lunchtime. In celebration of the occasion and to summon passengers from down below, the skipper gave a pull on the ship's bronze bell. "Fish chowder," he announced, "the best on the coast of Maine."

There have been many claims for fish chowder over the years, and it's anyone's guess who makes the best. Kenneth Roberts, the novelist, once wrote:

> Mystery has risen like a fog around Maine fish chowder. Some cooks argue that it can't be made properly without soiling eight or ten stew-pans, dishes and cauldrons. A few pontifically announce that salt pork should never be used; but many contend that pork not only should be used, but should be tried out separately, the liquid fat thrown away, and only the pork scraps added to the stew. There is also a large school of thought which insists that the head and backbone must be boiled separately, and the juice from them used as a basis for the chowder.

I'm not sure how many pans, dishes, and caldrons our cook used, or if and how salt pork was involved, but it was a fantastically good chowder—thick, fishy, and hot. We ate in

Weather permitting, lunch is served *al fresco*, with the top of the cabinhouse serving as a buffet table. The skipper has stepped away from the wheel for a moment to grab a quick mouthful and take a look at the chart at the same time. The yawlboat is rigged astern to help push the schooner in the light airs.

the lee of the cabinhouse, with a clear view of Vinalhaven and Hurricane islands, a couple of miles away.

Vinalhaven, the largest of the Fox Islands, once was one of the country's leading producers of building stone. Like several of the islands of lower Penobscot Bay—Dix, Hurricane, Deer, Crotch, and others—it had an almost unlimited supply of granite that was ideally suited to large-scale construction. It also had the proper deepwater harbors for shipping the stone.

The first quarry on Vinalhaven, a small one, was established in the 1820s; by the middle of the century, there were about a dozen small operations, working sometimes, closed often. But the building boom along the eastern seaboard following the Civil War dramatically changed what essentially had been a cottage industry. In 1871, Joseph R. Bodwell, a onetime governor of Maine, amalgamated several of the quarries into the Bodwell Granite Company, and Vinalhaven became a serious producer of stone until the company went out of business in 1919. Vinalhaven stone was used in hundreds of buildings, among them the Brooklyn Bridge; the Pilgrims' Monument in Plymouth, Massachusetts; and Grant's Tomb and the Cathedral of St. John the Divine in New York City. The main quarry, just outside Carvers Harbor, yielded a grade of blue-gray granite that was considered to be among the finest stone found anywhere in the United States.

So, too, the granite from nearby Hurricane Island, which can now be found all over the country, including the Museum of Fine Arts in Boston, the Customs House in New York, the Treasury Department in Washington, and the U.S. Naval Academy in Annapolis. When the island was bought for a mere fifty dollars by General Davis Tillson of Rockland, who established the Hurricane quarries in the early 1870s, there were only a handful of residents, but in short order the island had a regular town of perhaps 2,000 people, with several stores, boardinghouses, a school, a dance hall, and a church. It was a company town, run with an iron fist by General Tillson—known by the Finnish, Scottish, Irish, Swedish, and Yankee laborers as the "Lord of the Isles," and by the skilled Italian stonecutters as *"Bombasto Furioso."*

The quarries on Vinalhaven and Hurricane, as well as on most of the other quarrying islands, were hotbeds of radical politics; the behavior of the owners, who were noted for their manipulations and exploitations, saw to that. It was fertile territory for union organizers, and Penobscot Bay, of all places, was therefore well known around the country for its periodic labor wars, the most famous of which took place in 1892, "The Year of the Lockout," when the Granite Manufacturers Association fought dirty to break the principal stonecutters' union.

But it wasn't the labor movement that torpedoed the island quarry industry. It was simple economics: Other building materials from other places came into favor, and by World War I the quarries on Vinalhaven and Hurricane and everywhere else on the bay were in serious decline. Today, all the island quarries are silent, with the exception of a

The *Angelique*.

small operation on Crotch Island, next to the Deer Island Thorofare. Vinalhaven is now primarily an island of fishermen; Hurricane is the base of operations for the Outward Bound School, a camp for wilderness survival training.

The development of the quarries and their success at the height of their operations depended on the coasting vessels—at first small sloops, which were favored because it was easier to rig the derricks for loading and unloading the stone, and, in the later years, larger schooners. (Most so-called stone schooners carried their mainmasts farther aft than usual to accommodate the derricks.)

Schooners were built specifically for hauling stone, but just as many of them were converted from other uses, such as carrying lumber and cordwood. The Deer Isle quarries were noted for their converted fishing schooners—among them the *Accumulator*, the *Cordova*, the *Valparaiso*, and the *Black Warrior*—too used up for the extremes of the fishing banks but with enough life left for the stone trade. A stone schooner, however, couldn't be *too* used up. After all, nothing sinks faster than a wooden vessel packed to the deckbeams with paving blocks and building stone.

A loaded stone schooner, known on the bay as a "stone drogher," was a strange sight: to the untutored eye it looked much like a sinking ship. "I have seen the *Annie & Reuben* with something over 200 tons of stone aboard," wrote John Leavitt, "lying at Crotch Island wharf with the water flowing through the scuppers to the height of an inch or more on the main hatch coaming over the deck. This in a flat calm. Loaded in such fashion, the schooners resembled half-tide ledges when at sea, and it is sure the hatches were well battened down and the pumps going steadily the entire trip."

The last stone drogher built in Maine—indeed, one of the last sailing cargo vessels of any type built in the state—was the *Anna Sophia*, launched in Dennysville in 1923. But the last coaster to haul stone was the *Annie & Reuben*, which carried on into World War II, alternating stone with scrap iron for the war effort. Owned by the John L. Goss quarries in Stonington and built in Bath in 1891, she was wide, stout, and massively put together to stand up to the heaviest loads, most stowed in the hold, some on deck. Her usual run was from Penobscot Bay down to Boston, though on occasion she called on other New England ports. She was well known in Portland, as she used that city as a harbor of refuge. Residents with a view of the Portland roadstead considered the *Annie & Reuben* to be a barometer: If she was in port, they knew a storm was on the way.

Though a few schooners like the *Anna Sophia* and the *Annie & Reuben* carried stone well into the twentieth century, most of the stone droghers went out of business long before the quarries declined. They were forced out by a more reliable means of transportation: steam and diesel tugboats towing barges with much more capacity than the largest schooners in the trade.

Midafternoon found us barreling along with the wind almost dead astern and the seas building behind us with broad, foaming crests. The stern of the schooner would sink into

walnut cake, coffee, tea, the works. The cook tipped her hat to a standing ovation: she and the galley hand had put together the entire feast with only a cast-iron stove fueled with balks of split maple and oak and the occasional alder for fast heat.

Woodstove cooking. "It is a challenge," according to Dee Carstarphen, who was cook for several years on the passenger-schooner *Adventure*. "If you think you can slide your cake in the oven, dust your hands and that's that—wrong! The hottest spot is next to the fire box on the top shelf. When that cake browns, it must be turned, then moved away from the hot spot and finished up on the lower shelf to brown the bottom. No heat indicator or timer can help you here. You 'feel' the temperature and develop a gut sense about it."

They call the result "schooner food," virtually a generic term along the coast of Maine these days, and in essence it is good old down-home chow—no fancy sauces, no cute little arrangements, no reliance on exotic fruits and vegetables and spices from specialty shops, no fad-foods-of-the-month here. Meat, potatoes, fish, bread, coffee, pudding, summer squash—the type of food you get in lumber camps in the Maine woods, chuck wagons out in Wyoming, Pop's Diner down in Warwick, Rhode Island. Food with gusto. When you stand up after supper in the galley of a schooner with the smell of percolating coffee in the air, the kerosene lamps glowing, and the mate slicing off another slab of carrot cake with his rigging knife, you know you've had a *meal*—neither the salt meat or salt fish burgoo that was standard on the old coasting schooners nor the teeny-weeny *nouvelle cuisine* snacks in some of the tony restaurants ashore. What you need afterward is a little exercise.

So I took the skippers personal Whitehall pulling boat, a delicate little thing with spoon-bladed oars and bronze oarlocks, out for a row around the harbor, the tall spruce trees reflected in the dark water and a brace of deer grazing in a fisherman's yard. Meanwhile, the mate and the galley hand lowered the seine boat over the side of the schooner with the lifeboat falls for any of the passengers who wished to go ashore. Few of them had ever rowed before, and the boat clattered off to the darkening village like a wounded insect. From across the harbor on the Minturn side I could see them strolling up the single street, I could see the skipper, the mate, the cook, and the galley hand sharing a jug of wine on the main cabin house of the schooner, I could see the huge orange moon rising through the purple sky over Harbor Island, and I could hear the tide rising over the mussels beds.

III "Built by the Mile and Saved Off in Lengths"

The large Eastern coasting schooner was in many ways symbolic of the period between the Civil War and World War One, when American society was on the one hand irreversibly committed to a future of vast changes, while on the other still tied to traditions of ages past.
　　　　—William H. Bunting, *Steamers, Schooners, Cutters & Sloops*

When I was a boy, growing up on Cape Cod in the 1940s and 1950s, I spent a good part of my spare time hanging around the waterfront. I was a schizophrenic adolescent, torn between the pursuit of a higher calling, such as social service or the arts, and nautical monomania. Would I be a doctor or a clam digger, a concert violinist or a merchant mariner? It was a difficult time, made all the more difficult by the sights and sounds and smells of certain harbors—Provincetown, Chatham, Harwich, Woods Hole, Vineyard Haven, New Bedford—and the vision of sails on the horizon off Peaked Hill, the Chatham bars, Monomoy, and the Elizabeth Islands.

I was an incurable romantic who spent as much time studying the wooden hulks up on the shore of Wellfleet Harbor and the fishing draggers unloading their catches by the tumbledown wharves of Provincetown as I did reading Caesar and memorizing multiplication tables. I could conjugate verbs and play "The Flight of the Bumblebee" on the violin; cull littlenecks, cherrystones, and chowder quahogs with my eyes closed; and tell the difference between eastern- and western-rigged draggers at five miles.

Every once in a while in my longshore travels I would come across a coasting schooner laid up in a backwater or falling apart next to a wharf or waiting to be junked, sold foreign, or converted to a fried-clam takeout or some such thing. It was a crushing sight for a nautical monomaniac, proof positive that I was born too late for the Great Age of Sail. I had even missed the Lesser Age of Sail, that dark period between the world wars when a rather pathetic collection of aging and economically marginal vessels tried, with little success, to compete with the efficiencies and conveniences of the engine-powered vessel and the trucking industry.

Yet at the same time, I found those tired old vessels inspiring. Many of them had lived through the years of America's maritime ascendancy; if they could speak, they could talk about things I would never experience, events I could only read about in history books. I remember, for example, coming across the almost-sunken *Alice S. Wentworth* in Woods

A windjammer rendezvous in a cove off Eggemoggin Reach. A rare sight these days, such a gathering of coasters would have been commonplace in the early decades of this century. That's the *Grace Bailey* in the foreground.

Hole. Launched a hundred years earlier, in 1863, right in the heart of the Civil War, she had helped build New York City, carrying bricks on the Hudson from the brickyards upriver to the construction sites downriver. Later she went east to Maine, where she joined the general cargo trade. Her homeports were variously Wells, Kennebunk, Portland, Vineyard Haven, and New Bedford, and under the stewardship of Captains Arthur Stevens of Maine and Zebulon N. Tilton of Martha's Vineyard, she was an institution along the New England coast. Skippered by Captains Frederick Guild and Havilah Hawkins, she had carried passengers around Penobscot Bay in the early years of the Maine windjammer trade. She had seen the passage of generations—she was young when my grandfather's father was a young man—and there she lay before my very own eyes in Woods Hole, as broken down as a farm horse just this side of the glue factory. The scum may have been rising in her bilges and the moss may have been growing in the seams of her deck planking, but she was still the physical evidence of a vital part of America's maritime past.

The northeast coasting trade of old—the hauling of cargo from one port to another in wooden sailing vessels—never had the romance of carrying tea from China or wool from Australia or ivory from Africa, but it did have a peculiar hold on the psyches of some sailors, perhaps because it could be so exciting on the one hand and so mundane on the other. The yin and yang of the sailor's world. There would be periods of fast, pulse-pounding sailing in a near gale juxtaposed with quiet interludes in out-of-the-way ports, tricky navigation in the fog followed by wild weekends in Boston or New York. Deepwater sailing may have provided greater rewards in strange lands and exotic ports, but it involved days, weeks, months of boredom and sometimes terror on the empty ocean to get there. Coasting had its dull moments—and, occasionally, its terror—but the next port usually was only a few days away, and any seaman could live through that.

To the coastermen, the land was as important as the sea; home could be both the ship *and* the shore. Many were the sailors who split their time between a farm with cows, chickens, horses, and goats, and a schooner making short hops up and down the coast. (There were several sailors, for that matter, who took the farm with them. John Leavitt remembered a skipper who sailed with both his family and his livestock: "The former forecastle of his old packet, vacated when the deck hoisting engine replaced the larger crews, was a combination pigpen and henhouse, and the schooner was generally referred to as the 'floating barnyard.' It was claimed she was recognizable in a fog by the smell.")

The first coastermen were seagoing farmers, New England colonials who carried their produce in small craft (such as longboats and shallops) from saltwater farms and outlying villages to the developing seaports engaged in foreign commerce. As early as the 1670s, the regular business of coasting had been established, involving specialized vessels that would call on the various settlements to load cargoes for foreign trade in exchange for the necessities of life and to carry passengers along the coast in a time when overland travel, while not totally impossible, was at best extremely difficult. By the Revolutionary War, there was a vast fleet of coasting vessels—packets, general traders, lumber carriers, fish smacks, etc.—working not just what is now Maine, or Maine and Massachusetts, or Maine, Massachusetts, and New York, but the entire east coast, including all of the large rivers and many of the medium and small ones. This network extended from Canada to the Caribbean, with eastern coasters dominating trade in the latter region even after the Revolution, when such commerce was technically foreign.

The coasting trade, in fact, was essential to the development of the new United States, whose economy depended on trade among the individual states as well as with foreign nations. Deepwater sailing ships carried cargo across the oceans; coasting vessels carried it among the states. So important was the latter and so lucrative was the business that a series of laws was passed by the new nation to reserve the coasting trade for American vessels and American crews. In 1789, a tonnage tax was passed that discriminated against foreign vessels in domestic commerce. Later, the Embargo Act of 1808 and the American Navigation Act of 1817 forbade foreign-flag vessels from trading between ports in the United States. A British ship, for example, could deliver a cargo from London to Boston but could not load another cargo in Boston and carry it to New York. (The only deviation from this exclusionary policy came during the world wars as an emergency measure.)

The peacetime, post-Revolutionary years—especially those after the War of 1812 and again after the Civil War—witnessed an explosion of domestic waterborne commerce in relation to foreign commerce. (Some claimed protectionism was the cause: Since Americans had a monopoly on domestic commerce, they tended to invest more heavily in that.) As the years passed, the proportion of the American merchant marine devoted to the coasting trade increased, while that involved in foreign trade decreased. In 1838, the total tonnage of coasting vessels exceeded that of American foreign-trading vessels for the first time, the gap increasing as the decades passed; by the turn of the century, coasting tonnage was five times the foreign tonnage.

But for sailors there was a problem. Within the coastal fleet itself, another statistical bellwether developed during the nineteenth century: Sail was giving way to steam and, in the twentieth century, to diesel. By the turn of the century, mechanical power was slightly ahead of sail; in 1907, when the greatest amount of coastal sail tonnage in the United States was recorded, sail still amounted to less than 40 percent of the total. Four decades later, the percentage of sail was so small as to be hardly worth calculating. Today, with the exception of a handful of passenger vessels around the coasts and a dwindling fleet of oyster dredgers on Chesapeake Bay, commercial sail in America—coastal or foreign—is dead.

✷

It was a grand old time while it lasted. The major, minor, and even inconsequential ports of the United States, primarily on the east coast but elsewhere as well, including the Great Lakes, were awash with sailing vessels during the nineteenth century and early decades of the twentieth. Nobody has compiled an accurate count of the numbers and probably nobody will, but anyone who has read contemporary descriptions written by the few people who paid attention to such things (little public notice was given the coasting fleet, as it was so commonplace) or has seen photographs of eastern harbors in, say, 1882 or 1905, will understand. I have on hand, for example, a photograph of a small corner of Portland Harbor on a windless summer day at the turn of the century: Sixteen two-masted coasting schooners are awaiting a breeze. In William Bunting's *Portrait of a Port* is a magnificent photograph of Boston Harbor on a typical day in the early 1870s showing more than eighty coasting vessels—from sloops through multimasted schooners—at anchor.

Charlie York, a fisherman from Harpswell, Maine, remembered similar scenes along the coast in the early decades of this century:

> Outside Half-Way Rock you might see coasters with barrels of lime from Thomaston, granite or pavin' stone from Vinalhaven, ice from the Kennebec, lumber and laths or Aroostook potatoes from Bangor, Stark and Baldwin apples from saltwater farms, cordwood from little villages along the shore. It was a pretty sight after a storm, when the schooners had been layin' up in some safe harbor. I've seen thirty or forty of them vessels within an area of a square mile, white sails spread to the wind, standin' out across Casco Bay.

Though vessels of all rigs served as coasters—including square-riggers such as brigs, brigantines, barks, barkentines, and ships—the rig of choice on the eastern seaboard after about 1840 was the schooner. By the late nineteenth century, almost all coasters were schooner-rigged, and during the last years of the cargo-carrying era, the schooner was universal. There were several reasons for this, all based on economics: The schooner rig was simpler than the square rig, requiring less rope, fewer spars, and less hardware than a comparably sized square-rigger. A simpler rig required fewer sailors to handle the vessel. And, most important, the schooner rig was more weatherly than the square rig: schooners could sail closer to the wind, which meant they generally could make better time along the coast and could be maneuvered more easily in rivers and harbors and other tight

Boston Harbor on a typical day in the latter part of the nineteenth century, with perhaps eighty coasting vessels at anchor. Long Wharf to the left, Central Wharf in the middle, India Wharf to the right.

waterways. In short, schooners could make more trips per year at less expense and therefore produce more income and keep a larger proportion of it.

Of course, in competition with steamships, which were much in evidence during the coasting schooner's zenith, the schooner's strengths vis-à-vis the square-rigger's didn't count for much. What did count was no engineroom and no fuel bunkers and therefore ample space in the hull for cargo, and no fuel bill to pay. The wind, after all, was free. When time and speed and regularity of delivery were of the essence, steamers had a tremendous advantage over coasting schooners, but when it came to hauling bulk cargo, such as coal and lumber—cargoes that would be just as fresh whenever they were delivered, now or a week from now—the schooner was king. The steamers took most of the passengers and the high-grade freight (the perishables and the manufactured goods); the schooners carried the raw materials.

✦

The age of the coasting schooner, when viewed from afar, can best be described in general terms as a period of a century and a half that was bracketed by an era of small two-masted schooners at the beginning and the end, and dominated by huge multimasted schooners in the middle. What's more, it was an era during which the absolute limits of the size, power, and economics of the wooden hull were tested, and tested, and tested again and again. How big could a schooner be? How many masts could she carry? How simple could the rig be made? What were the risks in building wooden vessels so huge that they pushed the outer limits of the engineering knowledge of the time?

In general, two types of schooner hull were in favor. One was rather deep, much like that of the medium clippers designed for ocean passages. (Many of the deep-bodied schooners actually sailed foreign besides trading coastwise.) The other was quite shallow and wide to enable the vessels to carry deck loads and sail safely in the thin waters of the coast, especially the shoals around Cape Cod and, of course, the less-than-deepwater harbors of the mid-Atlantic states and the South. Most, but not all, of the latter type were fitted with centerboards so the vessels could get a better grip on the water. For example, the five-master *Governor Ames*, a very large coasting schooner, was very shallow in relation to her length and therefore was fitted with a centerboard. (One of her masts had to be offset from the centerline of the hull to make room for the massive centerboard trunk, giving the *Ames* an odd look when viewed from dead forward or aft.)

In the early days of the schooner era, when the two-master was the archetypal coaster, the practical dimensions of the hull were determined by the size of the sails. As the schooner owners tried to compete with steam the only way they could—by increasing the capacity of their vessels to carry bulk cargoes—they came up against the central matter of safety: The larger the hull, the larger the sail area required to drive it; the larger the fore-and-aft sails, the more difficult they were to reef or furl in a blow. There was a point in its size when the two-masted schooner was too dangerous for its crew.

A smart builder, name unknown, developed a solution and in the process opened a gate

in schooner design consciousness that wouldn't be closed until after World War I: Don't increase the sail area of larger schooners by increasing the size of the individual sails; do it by increasing the number of sails and the number of masts. So the small two-master evolved into the large three-master and then the larger four-master, the even larger five-master, and the mammoth six-master. By the time coastal sail had reached its apogee, just after the turn of the century, a seven-masted behemoth, the *Thomas W. Lawson*, had been launched.

As in all matters nautical, there has been endless disagreement about the origin of the first three-masted schooner. Most historians suggest that the rig dates from the 1820s or 1830s; certainly there are several shipbuilding towns that can point to a three-master having been built there during that period. Residents of Mathews County, Virginia, recall the three-masted schooner *Pocahontas* of 1827. Ellsworth, Maine, stakes its claim on two small three-masters, the *Aurora* and the *Fame*, of 1831.

Yet according to Howard Chapelle, one of the foremost historians of naval architecture, the rig goes back to the very beginning of the nineteenth century or even earlier, long before the schooner came to dominate the coasting trade. There are other observers who would make the claim that the modern three-master was invented much later; mid-century or even after the Civil War. George Wasson, for example, suggested that the *David Wasson*, built by his grandfather on Penobscot Bay in 1867, was one of the first, if not the first, three-master built in New England. But Wasson was splitting hairs. He admitted that there were earlier three-masters, such as the *Aurora* and the *Fame*, but maintained they were all old-fashioned topsail schooners—that is, they carried squaresails in addition to fore-and-aft sails on their foremasts. (One of the fundamentals of the definition of a modern schooner is that all sails must be rigged fore-and-aft.)

Argue about the where and the when of the first three-master all you want. The core of the matter is that once the advantages of the type became well known, three-masted coasters came off the shipways by the hundreds, reaching their peak during the 1880s, when, as a saying of the time had it, they were "built by the mile and sawed off in lengths to suit the owners' pleasure." In 1883 alone, at least 138 three-masters were built on the Atlantic coast, more than half of those in New England. The largest was the *Bradford C. French*, 920 tons, built in Kennebunkport, Maine, in 1884.

The down-east three-master was known for its beauty and balance of proportion, having neither the chunkiness of many of the two-masters nor the out-of-scale excess of the four-, five-, six-, and seven-posters. In a letter home, A.J. Green, an Englishman, described a typical three-master of 272 tons built at Bucksport, Maine, in 1882:

> ...A neighbor arrived a few days ago, a handsome "down east" schooner (three masted) called the *Susie P. Oliver*. Please note the initial letter, without which an American name would be incomplete. Almost all American vessels are named after some individual (an abominably tasteless fashion), and every name must of necessity include the initial, as Joel F. Hopkins, Amanda K. Jones. They are great institutions, these same schooners, for owing to their simplicity of rig, they can sail a vessel of 900 tons capacity with eight hands all told.

The archetypal coaster of both the early and later days of the schooner era. This is the *Stephen Taber* out of Rockland.

They sail well, shift without ballast, use but little gear, and rarely exceed thirteen feet in draught. Perhaps the first thing that strikes a stranger's eye is their enormous beam. This schooner alongside of us is much less tonnage than the *Mertola* but her beam is thirty-five feet, the *Mertola*'s being twenty-nine feet. One would think that so much breadth with so little depth would make them very skittish in a seaway, and be terribly severe on the masts, but they seem to get along all right, and undoubtedly sail like foam balls. Their cabin accommodations make me quite envious. Imagine, my sea-faring friends, a skipper having a private sitting-room, ten feet by ten feet, with spare rooms off it; a bedroom abaft, ten feet by seven feet; large bathroom and companion way—all in his own quarters; while on the fore side of his bulkhead is a cabin, ten by twelve; with mates' berths, pantry, steward's room, etc. on each side.

❋

Although schooners were built on all coasts, most of the major shipyards were in New England, with the center of activity being the state of Maine. In such towns as Bath, Yarmouth, Waldoboro, Rockland, Camden, Searsport, Ellsworth, and those in between, the din of saws, hammers, adzes, and caulking mallets was part of the local scene, especially after the Civil War, when the bulk of the coasting fleet was constructed. Maine had a seafaring tradition going back to the first white settlers, deepwater harbors with steep shores (just the thing for launching huge vessels), and a skilled labor force of shipwrights, caulkers, blacksmiths, dubbers, loftsmen, and riggers, men who didn't merely build ships—they *loved* to build ships, and they didn't charge an arm and a leg for the privilege.

Until the 1880s, the Maine shipyards specializing in large wooden vessels concentrated on deepwater square-riggers, the clippers during their intense but brief maritime heyday in midcentury, and then the more practical medium clippers, the Maine style of which came to be known around the world as "Down Easters." But after the Civil War insurance rates were higher for wooden ships in foreign commerce than for those of iron and steel, making them less competitive. Faced with declining orders for their most important product, the Maine yards shifted their attention to multimasted coasting schooners.

Maine at the time was a land of maritime innovation, a place where many of the technological improvements in the shipbuilding industry were first worked out, not the least of which was the steam-powered windlass. The first coasting schooner to be favored by the invention was the three-master *Charles A. Briggs* in 1879. The steam windlass was used to hoist the sails, raise the heavy anchor, load and discharge cargo, and even pump the bilges. Jobs that had previously required a large crew of sailors and stevedores now needed only a handful, and the main remaining barrier to constructing ever-larger schooners—the operating expense of a large crew—was eliminated. Schooners in the 200- to 300-foot range became common. Square-riggers of that size would have required crews of up to 100 men; the schooners scraped by with fifteen or fewer, including the officers.

Perhaps the first three-masted schooner can't be attributed to the state of Maine, though nobody has been able to prove convincingly otherwise, but the four-, five-, and six-

The *Domino Effect*, ex-*Victory Chimes*, at anchor with her awnings rigged. The last three-masted schooner on the coast, she was built in 1900 in Bethel, Delaware, as the *Edwin and Maude*. Her proportions are not nearly as elegant as the classic three-masters, as she was designed to be able to fit through the Chesapeake and Delaware Canal.

masters can be. The first four-master, the *William L. White*, was built in Bath in 1879, the year of the steam windlass. By the time the last four-master, the *Josiah B. Chase*, was built in 1921, approximately 460 had been constructed, the vast majority in Maine yards. The largest, at more than 2,000 tons, the *Northland*, was built in Rockland in 1906. The first five-master, the *Governor Ames*, was built in Waldoboro in 1888. A total of fifty-six, all but four built in Maine, were constructed before the big-schooner era ended. The first six-master, the *George W. Wells*, was launched in Camden in 1900. Of the grand total of nine six-masters, seven were constructed at the Percy & Small Shipyard in Bath, including the largest of all, the great *Wyoming*, which could carry a single load of 6,000 tons of coal.

Shipbuilding innovations notwithstanding, there is a practical limit to the size of wooden hulls, and the six-masters reached it. Some would say they exceeded it. They were so large, in fact, that the shipwrights had to go to great lengths to reinforce the schooner's structures to keep them from hogging—a condition in which the ends of the vessel, with less buoyancy than the middle, would tend over time to droop from their own weight. A massive, reinforced backbone was required; in addition, the sheer—the fore-and-aft sweep of the topsides—was accentuated so the ends, when they did droop, wouldn't produce a reverse sheer, spoiling the schooner's looks and, more important, reducing her seakeeping abilities.

They were magnificent vessels, the six-masted coasters, but when you get right down to it, they were too much, too late. Designed to be the last word in the efficient, cheap transport of bulk cargoes—coal and lumber, for the most part—they proved to be difficult to handle in certain critical situations, especially when sailing light, and they became uneconomical in just a few years' time. What's more, they and the other multimasted schooners became too expensive to build. Their construction consumed mountains of wood, and much of the premium stock that was required had to be hauled by other schooners over long distances. Oak for the frames came from all over the eastern seaboard, hard pine for the planking came from the South, hackmatack for the knees came from Nova Scotia, and pine for the masts and spars came from as far away as Oregon. Shipyard labor may still have been cheap, but materials no longer were.

The era of the six-master lasted a mere quarter of a century from the launching of the *George W. Wells* to the burning of the *Edward J. Lawrence*, the last of the type, at Portland just after Christmas, 1925. Business for all of the big multimasted coasting schooners was dead by that time; indeed, it was in serious decline before 1910. Pushed aside by steam freighters and colliers that could virtually guarantee delivery of their cargoes on time, every time, they had become dinosaurs of the coast. In the new, twentieth century, shipowners soon discovered that time was more important than cheap cargo fees, that people were willing to pay a premium for prompt delivery, that the quickening pace ashore left little room for the casuals of the sea. Many of the big schooners were laid up just a few years after they were built. Later, in the 1930s, quite a few had their rigs cut down and were converted to the very tug-towed barges that had provided such devastating competition for their sisters. They made a forlorn sight, their once-beautiful hulls

Coasting schooners at anchor in the fall of 1900 in Boston's outer harbor, awaiting their turn at the docks. The five-masters in the foreground are (left) the *William C. Carnegie* of Portland and the *Jennie French Potter* of New York. They are deeply laden with coal.

blackened with coal dust, lying against loading wharves in Norfolk, Virginia; tethered in long strings behind powerful coastal tugs in the Cape Cod Canal; moored to stake boats in eastern ports.

There was a brief flurry of activity for the coasting schooners during World War I, when everything that floated (some just barely) was pressed into service. Shortages of ships, coastal and deepwater, forced freight rates higher and higher, and investors saw an opportunity to make a quick killing. Shipyards across the nation cranked out vessels of all types, including hundreds of schooners—more than a hundred four-masters in the period 1916 to 1920, for example.

But the boom didn't last. The wartime shortage of ships became a peacetime glut, and the bottom fell out of the schooner trade in the space of a year. In 1920, the freight rate for coal from Norfolk to Boston was three dollars a ton; in 1921, it was a dollar. The Great Age of Coastal Sail was over.

Enter the Lesser Age, for while by definition in a progressive society all things must pass, some things take longer to pass than others. Years ago, mechanical tractors were proven to be economically superior to beasts of burden, but even today a few farmers still plow their fields with draft horses. In the 1940s and 1950s, motor trucks had long since been proven better than horses and wagons, yet in Boston, for example, there were peddlers and junk pickers with reins in their hands. There may no longer have been big money to be made in coastal sail after World War I, but there was small money, and hundreds of

The *Stephen Taber* (left) and *Mary Day* (right) in a calm, being pushed along slowly by their yawlboats. The *Taber*, built in 1871, is one of the oldest commercial sailing vessels in America. The *Mary Day*, built in 1961, is one of a handful of schooners built especially for the passenger trade.

schooners still in sound condition could be had for a song. There were also two classes of people indispensable to a lingering marginal trade: those who were so set in their ways that they would never change, no matter what; and those whose vision was so clouded with a romantic haze that economics had little to do with the way they chose to make a living.

Not that you couldn't make a living in coasting schooners after the war. There still were cargoes for some of the larger schooners that hung on into the 1930s: lumber, coal for the communities served by neither the railroads nor the tug-barge combinations, salt for the fishing fleets, that type of thing. If an owner bought his schooner at a creditor's auction; if he skimped on maintenance, making only those repairs affecting the ability of the vessel to stay afloat and forgetting about the rest; if he hired sailors who couldn't get a job elsewhere or who didn't want a job elsewhere or who were young and driven by the urge to escape to the sea and therefore would accept wages considered substandard by indigent hod carriers; if he pinched every penny he got from the miserly shipping agents; if he browbeat his skipper to get underway and stay underway whatever the weather, whether prudent mariners thought it foolhardy or not, he just might be able to make schoonering a paying proposition. Nothing like the kind of money the owners had been making in the last two decades of the nineteenth century, but enough to get by. It was difficult, but it could be done.

The Great Depression, however, finally did them in. The remaining big schooners were laid up in the hopes of better days that never came, or sold at auction to be stripped and converted to restaurants or nightclubs or other pie-in-the-sky schemes. The *Charles D. Stanford*, built during the boom years of World War I for $100,000, sold in 1931 for $5,000. Nine schooners from the fleet of the New England Maritime Company, which went bankrupt in 1931, went for less than $14,000. That's $1,500 a schooner.

It was easier for the smaller schooners, though still no piece of cake. While they had suffered from arrested development during the years of the huge four-, five- and six-posters, the little two- and three-masters were still making their way along the coast, especially in Maine, where old ways, no matter the era, traditionally die hard. They specialized in forgotten cargoes to ports so obscure that even the burgeoning trucking industry couldn't be bothered. Cans to the sardine packers, salt to the fish plants, pulpwood to the paper factories, staples to the little towns in the hinterlands connected to the sea by tidal rivers and creeks, scrap metal to the dealers in Boston, Providence, New York, and other metropolises near and far. The little coasters were cheap to buy and cheaper to operate, requiring only a few able-bodied hands and minimal fuel for the make-and-break donkey engines powering the winches, their only nod to modern times.

Few two- or three-masters were built after the turn of the century, and only a handful after World War I. There were too many used schooners available at too cheap a price to make new construction economically feasible. Why build a new schooner when you could have your pick of the older ones for a few hundred dollars, drive her hard until she was all used up, throw her away, buy another one, and do it all over again?

The last cargo-carrying coasting schooner built in the state of Maine, an act of faith if ever there was one, was the *Endeavor*, a two-master launched in Stonington in 1938. (Actually, there was another, the *John F. Leavitt*, built at Thomaston in 1979, but she sank before she could deliver her first cargo.) The *Endeavor* was skippered by Albert Shepard, whose previous schooner, the *Enterprise*, eventually was converted to a cruise schooner. She carried salt fish to Gloucester from the ports of down-east Maine, salt and coal from Portland to out-of-the-way down-east communities and some of the isolated islands, and any other cargoes she could cadge together. Not that many cargoes were available; not that there was much competition for those that were.

The majority of the small schooners left in the trade were old, and some were positively ancient. The oldest in active use before World War I was the schooner *Polly*, a little 48-ton two-master built as a sloop in 1805 at Amesbury, Massachusetts. She had an old-fashioned high poop deck and bluff bows, and it was rumored she had served as a privateer during the War of 1812 (subsequent research suggests that was unlikely). She was rebuilt as a schooner in Blue Hill, Maine, in 1861, and worked the New England coast from Connecticut to Maine, although her last years seem to have been primarily in Massachusetts and Maine waters. She carried lumber, pulpwood, lime, stone, and anything else that would keep her going.

Most of the oldest schooners at work between the world wars were built in the mid-1800s; a few were pushing the century mark when they carried their last cargoes. Among them were the *William H. Jewell*, launched at Nyack, New York, in 1853; the *William C. Pendleton*, Westerly, Rhode Island, 1857; the *William Keene*, Damariscotta, Maine, 1866.

And then there was the venerable *Stephen Taber*, launched in Glenwood, New York, in 1871. Originally a Hudson River brick schooner, the 63-foot *Taber* eventually came to Maine and carried general cargoes in the Penobscot Bay region. By the mid-1930s, she was a tired old vessel with a hogged sheer, a prime candidate for a mudflat burial. But Captain Fred Wood of Orland, Maine, was looking for a vessel, and the *Taber* was available cheap, so Wood took a chance and rebuilt her himself on the shore near the mouth of the Penobscot River. Until 1943, the *Taber* carried pulpwood from the islands in the bay to the paper mills on the Penobscot River, until even that mundane task proved to be unprofitable and she had to find another. She was bought by Captain Frederick B. Guild of Castine in 1946 and converted to the passenger trade in company with her fellow former bricker, the *Alice S. Wentworth*.

The *Stephen Taber* works the bay to this day, not quite the oldest commercial sailing vessel in the United States—the *Lewis R. French* beats her by a few months—but definitely the oldest in continuous service, an achievement that puts her way ahead of the five-master *Governor Ames* and the six-master *Wyoming* and all the rest of the great schooners of the Golden Age of Coasting.

IV *Many Cargoes*

…I always had a contented feeling when coming back to the quiet ship, which once away from land became a little world of her own. Politics, murder, weddings and deaths meant as little to us as the breakfast food ads the skipper would listen to while tuning in for his morning weather report. We were healthy, usually happy … and there was always plenty of work aside from steering and handling sail to keep us out of mischief.
—Francis E. Bowker, *Blue Water Coaster*

I awoke early Tuesday morning, just before dawn, to the sound of a footfall directly above. My cabin was in the after quarter of the schooner; the overhead was the underside of the quarterdeck, next to the binnacle. With the exception of the insomniac on deck—the skipper? the mate checking the painter of the rowboat trailing off astern? a passenger watching the morning stars?—no one else was up and about. I could hear gulls in the distance and water gurgling against the oak planking next to my ear. As time passed and dawn broke, a shaft of light from a thick prism of glass set in a bronze ring partially illuminated the tiny compartment; I could see my yellow foulweather jacket at the foot of the bunk, my boots by the door, the washbasin on a stand in the corner.

A nearby fishing boat fired up its engine and got underway, the thump of its pistons becoming louder and louder as it passed along our starboard side and softer and softer as it receded into the distance. The schooner rolled slightly from the wake and then settled back. The sensation was of an incredibly comfortable easiness, untroubled quiescence, the paradox of motion in a state of motionlessness.

There's magic in the early morning aboard a coasting schooner in a quiet anchorage. "…Waking in the morning is different from what it is ashore," wrote John Leavitt. He continued:

> There is no struggling up uncomprehendingly from the maze of sleep, sodden and bewildered. Wakefulness comes, slow or fast, with the dawn, and with it, the pleasant awareness of familiar sounds and smells. There is the muted lapping of water against the hull and the hum of wind in the rigging. If there is much wind, the slapping of the halyards against the mast and the rumble of the taut anchor chain tells of it. The lingering scent of wood smoke mingles with the smell of pine and spruce lumber, spiced with a whiff of Stockholm tar from the oakum and marlin stowed in the lockers.

"The schooner rolled slightly from the wake and then settled back. The sensation was of an incredibly comfortable easiness, untroubled quiescence, the paradox of motion in a state of motionlessness." The *American Eagle.*

I pulled on my clothes, grabbed a peach from a bowl in the main cabin, and climbed the companionway ladder to the deck. We had no wind. The sun was climbing the back of a hill behind Minturn, its rays gilding the topmasts and reflecting off the second-story windows of the fishermen's houses in the tiny town of Swans Island. There was dew on the cabinhouse and a giant cobweb on the varnished skylight and verdigris on the clapper of the polished bronze bell. The air, typical of a Maine September, was cool, not quite sharp as in the heart of the fall but with just the barest hint of an edge. Autumn was approaching.

The cook's helper was sitting on one of the life-jacket lockers, cleaning strawberries and throwing the hulls over the side. She was nineteen years old, a native of "The County"— Aroostook County, the vast northern crown of Maine. Aroostook is one of those mythical areas of the state, rivaling "Down East" for its image of wilderness and the freedom of the frontier. Most of it is as far from the sea as Vermont. A land of forests and potato fields, The County has its own topography, its own culture, its own dialects, its own ethos, and its own paradoxical mix, bred by isolation, of unfettered individualism and tight community. It has the reputation of being a lingering bastion of New England hominess untouched by the sins of Boston and New York, a Norman Rockwell kind of place where the girls have freckled faces and the pie is thick with fruit and the land is abundant and cheap.

The County is an easy place to love and a tough place to leave. A motherland—a heartland—its natives think of themselves as different in certain indefinable respects, and, if they move away, they have a difficult time adjusting to a new locale, even if it is no farther away than Bangor or Berlin, New Hampshire. Merely the invocation of Aroostook's name can put a faraway, romantic look in the eye of a native gone wandering.

The cook's helper, an archetypal County farm girl with sky-blue eyes and strawberry-blond hair, was deep in her own struggle with the pull of Aroostook. She left home after high school for the University of Maine but dropped out during her freshman year "because I didn't know why I was there." She wanted to go home but thought she should see the world first. She wandered down to the coast, heard through the grapevine that there were job opportunities on the windjammers, and walked in the right door at just the moment when our schooner's skipper was drawing up the crew list for the coming season.

"He asked me if I minded peeling potatoes and stoking a woodstove," she said. "I told him I was from a potato farm. I also told him we heated with wood. He asked me if I could sing, and I told him that I could do that and play the guitar, too."

The skipper hired her on the spot, even though she didn't know a coasting schooner from a hay rake. It's one thing for a skipper to find a hand willing to work long hours at low pay in cramped conditions; it's frosting on the cake to find one who can pick out the chords for "Shenandoah" or "Blow the Man Down."

The nights are long on a schooner tucked into an empty cove miles away from bright lights and video rental stores. Homemade music, not to mention Scrabble and gin rummy, goes a long way in filling the entertainment void. The skipper played the pump organ and had a fine bass, the mate blew a mean blues harp and had a so-so tenor, and the cook sang alto. With the cook's helper's skills on the guitar and a soprano that could bring tears to your eyes, our schooner, though it couldn't hold a candle to the Village Gate, was still the most musically accomplished vessel in the fleet.

At six o'clock in the morning, there wasn't much going on in Burnt Coat Harbor. The cook climbed partway up the companionway ladder and pushed a tray with coffee, sugar, cream, and thick, white, navy-style mugs onto the deck. The few passengers who were up and about pounced on it as if they had been lost in a desert and this was the first liquid they had seen for weeks.

If there was one constant on our schooner, it had to be coffee. No matter the time of day or night, there was a pot on the galley stove; long before it was empty, another full one was perking along beside it. Coffee was traditional even on the old cargo coasters, where the sailors called it "ship's tea" and boiled the beans cowboy style. A crew could get along without fresh vegetables for long periods, without meat, with wet clothing and water-soaked bunks, but they could become near-mutinous without coffee, the best beverage for a jump-start in the morning, warmth during the day, and companionship during the long watches at night.

A couple of years ago, one of the Camden schooners left port on a Monday morning with

Coffee, and
plenty of it.
The galley of the
Lewis R. French.

the food pantry full but only a single one-pound can of coffee aboard, enough to last for about half a day. The cook thought the helper had brought the coffee supply, the helper thought it had been the cook, and the skipper and the mate had been too busy taking care of other matters to notice. The schooner was somewhere out in East Penobscot Bay, miles from the nearest store, when the terrible shortage was discovered. There were no deleted expletives that afternoon down in the galley. They were right out in the open where you could keep track of them. (The cook's helper, of course, was allowed to accept full blame for the disaster.)

The cook tried all sorts of alternatives, none of which came even close to replicating the experience of a "mug-up" of java. Tea didn't work. A can of "cereal beverage" left behind by an English eccentric had no effect. Celestial Seasonings' Morning Thunder ("When your get-up-and-go won't, Morning Thunder will") didn't even come close. The cook stopped talking to the galley hand, the mate took to chewing tobacco, most of the passengers became sullen and distracted, and even the skipper, noted for his joviality, went crank. No relief came for two days—until the schooner put into Stonington to pick up a crate of lobsters for the evening meal and a case of Maxwell House for the rest of the week. The first pot of coffee was brewed and consumed long before the water for the lobsters came to a boil.

We were amply fixed on our schooner. I borrowed a thermos from the cook, filled it with a good slug of steaming black coffee, and rowed ashore for a walk before breakfast. I found a town that wasn't a town. There were houses clustered in a village and a few ramshackle piers angling this way and that out into the harbor, but there were no people, no signs of life except a lobster fisherman stacking traps on the shore and an ancient dog nosing around a bait barrel. None of the hustle and bustle associated with life in a town, no automobiles coming and going, no lawn mowers or garbage collectors or paperboys bicycling past the houses and throwing newspapers at the front porches.

The most exciting sight was a down-at-the-heels boatyard with a sign that was more of a warning than an invitation: Boats Hauled and Stored at the Owner's Risk. And at some risk! Few of the boats were upright. Most were lying on their sides with weeds growing through their planks; one was tilted headfirst down an embankment toward the water. At the end of one of the piers was an old boat with peeling paint. "That's the *Maine Queen*," said the lone lobster fisherman. "She used to be a sardine carrier, hauled sardines from the boats that caught 'em to the canneries. Now she's owned by Baitbag Pete. Carries bait for the fishermen. Don't get too close to her. She's ranker 'n an old boot."

Across the still water came the ring of the ship's bell announcing breakfast. I rowed back to the schooner with a harbor seal swimming in my wake. He would poke his head up just behind the stern of the rowboat and stare at me like an old man studying a chess move, then duck down and reappear a few moments later farther astern. Some of the passengers spotted the seal and ran below for their cameras. One fellow hauled out a video camera and ground away as I circled the schooner and made my landing at the boarding ladder.

"There were no people, no signs of life....None of the hustle and bustle associated with life in a town, no automobiles coming and going, no lawn mowers or garbage collectors or paperboys."

What can I say? Down in the galley at the breakfast table, the passengers, to a one, looked absolutely fantastic. Gone was the wan, pasty-white flesh of the office manager and the medical technician; departed was the tension of the Boston cop and the woman who managed the restaurant trade magazine; absent were the bored expressions of the shoe salesman and the advertising copywriter. The men looked as if they could run for a week in the woods with Natty Bumppo and the last of the Mohicans and not get tired; the women looked as if they had bathed in the fountain of youth. Ruddy complexions, pink cheeks, smile lines at the corners of eyes and laughter to go with them. Those who had traces of sunburn glowed in the dimness of the light. A day in the sun, an evening at peace in the cradle of the deep, a morning that came with the simple pleasures of a washbasin and a bar of Ivory soap and soft water from the cask up on deck. At once it became difficult to remember exactly what life was like before we had cast off the dock-lines back in Rockland.

Breakfast of coffee, eggs, coffee, homemade biscuits, coffee, pancakes, coffee, French toast, coffee, sausage and bacon, coffee. It was a wonder anybody had the strength to get up from the table. Wired from the caffeine? If we had had a generator on board, we could have hooked up everybody and produced enough juice to operate the ship-to-shore radio for a month.

The skipper rapped on the side of his glass with a spoon. "You folks finally look like human beings," he said. "Let's go sailing!"

✵

Which was all well and good to say, but there was much to be done beforehand. While the skipper took the yawlboat ashore and ambled up the road to say hello to an old friend ("He has photographs of some of the old hay schooners," he said before he left, with the tone of voice one would use when discussing a national treasure), the mate organized the work parties.

"No one is expected to work when they pay for their vacation," he announced, "but assistance would be appreciated."

It was a Tom Sawyer deal. In almost no time at all, a bunch of otherwise grown-up, intelligent lawyers, doctors, and pillars of industry and science were convinced that it was an honor and a privilege to pump the bilges, wash the joinerwork, oil the anchor winch, and polish the brass. I took off my sneakers and rolled up my dungarees. My great good fortune was to be allowed to scrub the deck with a long-handled brush while the mate hauled salt water from over the side with a bucket at the end of a knotted lanyard and sloshed it into the corners.

Washing down the deck with salt water, morning and evening, is a practical tradition on wooden vessels. It cleans the deck and washes the grit out of the seams and helps preserve the vessel. In simple terms, the skin of a wooden ship is constructed of planks set edge to edge. Cotton and oakum caulking held in place with a puttylike compound prevents water from seeping through the seams between the planks. Keep the seams wet,

vacationers to raise the sails. They will have managed to get the job done, working from aft forward, with less cursing and yelling but with more grunting and sweating.

"Okay, Mr. Mate," the skipper says, "break her free and let's get the hell out of here."

Yell at the galley hand to engage the winch clutch, curse the hose handler who's been paying more attention to the view than the muddy chain, lock the winch when the anchor ring reaches the hawsepipe, shut down the donkey engine, help sheet in the sails, back the jib to get the schooner's head to fall off, "fish and cat" the anchor (pull it to the cathead and lash one of the flukes to the rail), curse the leaking oil from the donkey engine, tell the cook she's better at baking bread than coiling halyards, recoil the halyards, stow a few odds and ends, report to the skipper that the schooner is squared away.

The wind was light from the south-southwest, which meant we would be beating out of Burnt Coat and either broad-reaching or running up into the bay. "Looks like a fair chance for Blue Hill Bay," the skipper said, and the mate nodded.

"Chance," pronounced by the down-easters with the English broad A, is an old coasting word for the ability to sail. With a fair chance, a vessel can sail with sheets eased—that is, off the wind—and go with the tide or stem a foul one. With a hard chance, she faces tough going in a headwind, a driving sea, and perhaps a foul tide. "No chance" is just that: without auxiliary power, the schooner must stay put. A vessel with no chance, facing an unfair wind or tide, or no wind, is waiting for a chance-along. If you should hear a coasterman say, "I was off Dice Head looking for a chance-along in a dead calm trying to make Castine and the tide was setting me up toward Fort Point," he was waiting for a fair wind that would be strong enough to overcome a foul tide running up East Penobscot Bay.

We departed the harbor the hard way, tacking out of the channel to weather the Sheriff Ledges, then headed off toward the northwest on a broad reach into Toothacher Bay. The *Mary Day* followed us out, but she towed with her yawlboat, sweating up her sails by the big bell buoy rocking in the swell off Harbor Island. She squared away toward the southeast.

The *Mary Day* was the first schooner in Maine to be built specifically for the passenger trade. Launched in 1962, she was designed by her first owner, Havilah Hawkins, Sr. (she is now owned by Captain Steve Cobb), and constructed in South Bristol, Maine, by Harvey Gamage, who is so celebrated as a shipwright that another cruise schooner, which sails mostly in southern New England waters, was named after him.

Captain Havilah Hawkins—"Buds" to his friends—had been in the windjammer business for twelve years when he sold his two schooners, the 63-foot *Stephen Taber* and the 76-foot *Alice S. Wentworth*, and ordered a new one from Gamage. He designed the *Mary Day* to look like a coasting schooner but laid her out with the comfort of the passengers in mind. He provided standing headroom in the cabins and sitting-up headroom in the bunks (a not-inconsiderable convenience when you think about waking up with a start in a bunk with only a foot or two of clearance), even sloped the cabin sides,

"With a fair chance, a vessel can sail with sheets eased— that is, off the wind—and go with the tide or stem a foul one." The *Mary Day*.

which made comfortable backrests for passengers on deck. But Hawkins was also a great believer in the rustic experience of the coasters, so he intentionally excluded running water and other modern indulgences and avoided all the trappings of a gold-plated yacht.

Our skipper was cut from the same cloth. "A coasting schooner is a coasting schooner," he said. "The *Mary Day* may not have carried real cargo like this one, but at least she looks as if she could have. A Maine schooner shouldn't be all gussied up like a yacht. Look at some of those vessels! They're floating motels. Hot showers. Flush toilets. Jesus, what a mess!"

A fast schooner, especially with both topsails set, the *Mary Day* made quite a sight roaring out on a broad reach into the Gulf of Maine. If you squinted your eyes just right and took on a 1920s frame of mind, you could see her outward bound for Lunenburg, Nova Scotia, with a hold full of salt for the bluenose Grand Banks fleet or off to Lubec, just this side of the Canadian border, with empty cans for a sardine plant.

Cargo: the great legitimizer. To many of the surviving coastermen from the pre–World War II days, a schooner isn't a schooner unless it is carrying cargo. Even some of those who were born too late for commercial sail feel that way. A schooner that has been converted to a yacht or to a passenger-carrying windjammer is somehow suspect—a "dude schooner," a "skinboat" for gullible fools and desperate men who will do anything to make a buck.

It's an interesting concept, especially if you consider that the cargoes of the coasting schooners didn't even come close to the romantic sort carried by deepwater sail. No spices from Java, tea from Ceylon, seal pelts from the Pribilofs, ivory from the Gold Coast. Nothing like that. The Maine coasters carried very unromantic cargoes, messy stuff that for the most part was ignored by the rest of the world. Coal, coke, lumber, stone, ice, salt, pulpwood, lime, dried fish, bait, hay. A schooner might carry coal on one trip and salt on another, which meant the hold had to be cleaned of the grit, dust, and dirt of the former before the latter could be stowed. It was a dirty business.

There were three types of coasting vessel in Maine waters during the last years of commercial sail. Bay coasters, relatively small vessels, operated mostly along the Maine coast, carrying pulpwood to the paper factories, cordwood to the lime kilns in Rockland, and general supplies to the isolated communities with no railroad service and poor roads. Boston coasters, medium-size schooners, traded between Boston and the Maine coast with such cargoes as lumber, stone, lime, and hay to the westward and coal, coke, and salt for the fishermen to the eastward. The third type, simply known as schooners or coasters, were large vessels sailing anywhere on the eastern seaboard—to New York, the Chesapeake, the Carolinas, even the Caribbean. Their outward-bound cargoes were typically ice, lumber, and stone; they would return with southern lumber (hard pine, oak, cypress), coal, and salt.

Our schooner and the *Mary Day*, if time could be turned back, would be bay or, at the most, Boston coasters. They weren't large enough to trade successfully much beyond Massachusetts. In fact, there isn't a schooner today in the entire windjammer fleet that

The *Victory Chimes*, now the
Domino Effect, stepping along
with a "good chance."
Relatively slow in comparison
to the rest of the fleet, she
needs a good breeze to keep
her going.

could. The three-masted ram schooner *Domino Effect*, ex–*Victory Chimes*, carrying passengers out of Rockland, originally from the Chesapeake Bay, theoretically has had the capacity for bigger-time coasting, but she is a slow, logy vessel that takes forever to get where she is going and just as long to return.

But every once in a while someone will get all worked up about the romance of carrying cargo under sail and want to do something about it. Build a wooden ship, get together a crew, load a cargo of something and take it somewhere, and prove to all the troglodytic cynics in the waterfront saloons that nineteenth-century economics can work in the twentieth. All you have to do is believe.

✵

The year was 1979 and the second great fuel crisis of the decade was in full swing. Motorists waited in line for hours for the privilege of buying a couple of gallons of gasoline at whatever outrageous price the suppliers felt like charging. Service-station workers were no longer known as Bob or Dick or Sid; they had become Misters overnight, with more power in the community than the manager of the bank or the president of the chamber of commerce. Hardware stores were stripped of woodstoves, chain saws, bucking horses, and splitting mauls by those who feared a slow, agonizing death by creeping hoarfrost in the coming winter. Apocalyptic futurists were talking about the paralysis of modern society, survival of the fittest, terror in the streets, doomsday. Alternative sources of energy (anything but petroleum) were the thing; R-factors and down-filled fireside reading bags became hot topics of conversation.

Edward Arthur ("Ned") Ackerman pounded his chest and declared that he was a "merchant-adventurer," the first of a new breed of real men who would spit in the eyes of the OPEC cartel and revive sail-powered cargo schooners, which had been dead for more than thirty years. Before a crowd of 2,500 cheering spectators, he rode his brand-new two-masted cargo schooner, the *John F. Leavitt*, down the launching ways at Roy Wallace's shipyard in Thomaston. She was the first of the type to be built on the coast of Maine since 1938. Ackerman was the toast of the town, the coast, the nation. He didn't mind telling anyone who was willing to listen that he not only knew what he was doing but knew more about it than anyone who came before and expected to come after. Here he was on the deck of his own coasting schooner, surrounded by a bunch of ignoramuses who still thought there was a future for internal-combustion engines, and he was perfectly poised—positioned—to become the King of Cargo. He was so sure the clock had been turned back that he already had the plans for a larger, three-masted schooner on the drawing board.

Ned Ackerman had no previous experience in the schooner business beyond a modest amount of pleasure sailing. A college teacher, a graduate student in medieval English, he had picked up a copy of *Wake of the Coasters* by John F. Leavitt in the early 1970s, and, by the time he finished reading it for the third time, had come under the thrall of humping cargo from port to port. Yes, there had been a mild energy crisis in 1973, and yes, there had been cautious speculation about the viability of commercial sail. but nobody. including Ackerman, believed the economics were such that trailer trucks, railroad cars, and motor vessels were in any danger of serious competition from schooners. All Ackerman wanted was a stout vessel of his own to fill any niches that might exist: a little lumber here, some stone there, and a few passengers to pick up the slack.

He wasn't the only one who was looking in that direction. The Apprenticeshop of the Bath Marine Museum (now the Maine Maritime Museum) had built a replica of a Tancook whaler, a small schooner formerly used in the Nova Scotia fishing industry, and was using it to carry cordwood from the mainland to some of the islands that were long on softwood (not so good for wood-heating purposes) and short on hardwood (great for wood heat). And down in Massachusetts, a couple of entrepreneurs had built a 40-foot scow sloop and were carrying general cargo from New Bedford to Martha's Vineyard and back.

Things might have worked out for Ackerman, but between the time he contracted with Roy Wallace for the construction of his schooner and when she was actually launched, the second oil crisis of the 1970s struck, and anyone who was doing anything that involved "free" energy—wind, solar, geothermal, etc.—became a national media hero, the toast of the alternative-energy movement. Every journalist and commentator who could cadge together enough gas for the trip was making the pilgrimage downeast to Thomaston to put

The brand-new schooner *John F. Leavitt* slides down the launching ways at Wallace's in Thomaston in 1979. A few months later on her maiden voyage she was abandoned at sea during a winter storm.

together stories that inevitably compared Ackerman with the shipmasters and shipowners of the Great Age of Sail. He was on television, the radio, in magazines and newspapers; he and his schooner were stars of at least two ongoing documentary movies.

The pressure of the public eye is a powerful force. Overnight a quiet operation that might or might not work became a high-powered David-beats-Goliath deal that not only was going to work, it *had* to work. The alternative-energy gurus applauded. *People* magazine loved it. The world was ready for it. Ned Ackerman, the medievalist-turned-romantic, became the romantic-turned-media-star with a streak of hubris that would, in a few short months, lead to his public humiliation.

The nub of the matter is that Ned Ackerman was inexperienced. Unlike the skippers of the cruise schooners, which were similar to the *John F. Leavitt* except in the nature of the cargo they carried, he didn't have to have a Coast Guard–issued license. The vessel was designed and constructed to come just barely behind the threshold of Coast Guard regulation and therefore not be subject to stringent rules about ballasting, bulkheads, loading, and manning. Even if Ackerman had been subject to Coast Guard licensing requirements, he would not have been allowed to sit down and take the exam because he didn't have the requisite sea time. Yet the rules had been circumvented in such a way that Ackerman could simply say he was a schoonerman and he would *be* a schoonerman. The result was tragic in almost all respects.

The *Leavitt* was launched in the summer of 1979, and the vessel was prepared for sea during the fall. In the press of publicity—with the media yelling, "Go, Ned, go!" and Ned strutting the quarterdeck like Ted Williams at the plate—Ackerman secured a cargo for Haiti from Boston in December. It was the worst possible time of year for a coasting passage under any circumstance, never mind in a new, untried schooner under the command of an inexperienced sailor.

The outcome was predictable. After a series of minor disasters en route to Quincy, Massachusetts, where the cargo was loaded (some say overloaded), the schooner ran into an Atlantic winter storm east of New York just after Christmas, and, after suffering a certain amount of damage, had to be abandoned. Thanks to the work of the Air National Guard, which helicoptered the crew off the vessel, there was no loss of life.

There are those who said the *Leavitt* would not have been lost if she had been in the hands of one of the capable skippers of the old days, such as Captain Zeb Tilton of the *Alice S. Wentworth* or Captain Parker Hall of the *George Cress*. There were others who said neither Tilton nor Hall would have been so foolhardy as to go offshore in a coasting schooner in the winter. But most of the talk revolved around the dashing of a dream that had been so close to realization. A romantic had tried to revive coastal cargo-carrying under sail and had failed tragically before the first shipment had been delivered.

✪

"I'm glad there are no eels trying to follow us today," the skipper said, pointing over the stern at the wake, which twisted from side to side behind us. "They'd break their backs!"

The cook had taken the wheel so the skipper could concentrate on the radiotelephone. He was talking to various schooners along the coast about the immediate weather conditions and the prognosis for the future. There was much back-and-forthing about where to be the next night, when the NOAA weather forecasters predicted high winds and rain from the edge of a tropical storm. There were the popular foulweather harbors, of course—Gilkey on Islesboro, Burnt Coat on Swans Island, Pulpit on North Haven—but there were also several harbors favored by the individual skippers, virtually their own personal harbors of refuge. They were loath to discuss them out loud on the radio waves lest other vessels get there first and lay claim to the best holding ground.

The passengers were all over the place, settling in to the rhythm of the day. There was the usual cluster around the skipper ("Did I ever tell you why the two rocks off Ship Island are called the Barges?...") and a bunch down in the galley, a pair playing cards in the lee of the fore cabinhouse, some reading, some watching the procession of islands on either side of the vessel, and some helping the mate, who had his Tom Sawyer operation going full bore.

The mate carried a notebook in the back pocket of his dungarees for keeping track of the endless chores that had to be done. Grease the stuffing box in the yawlboat, overhaul the topsail sheet, fix the boarding-ladder socket, varnish the main skylight, that type of thing. Anyone who was idle and didn't want to remain in that condition could ask the mate for a project. He would pull his notebook out of his pocket, study it for a while, look up and assess the abilities and sincerity of the questioner, and say something like, "Well, I was sort of keeping the job of polishing the brass binnacle to myself because it's so much fun, but if you promise to do it right and keep from getting the dirty polish on the woodwork, I'll let you have it."

We were sailing with a quartering breeze up Blue Hill Bay, Tinker Island to port and the vast bulk of Mount Desert to starboard. The schooner picked up dolphins off her bows and seals in her wake as we headed in toward Bartlett Narrows, a narrow passage between Bartlett Island and Mount Desert. There was a rush to the rail as we passed Hardwood Island, which could only be described as paradise on the coast of Maine. Dock, boathouse, farmhouse, barns, outbuildings, fields, orchards—a gentleman's farm served by an old World War II landing barge with a ramp at the bow and a tiny pilothouse perched on the stern.

We lost much of our wind in the narrows, just ghosting along surrounded by dark spruces, green-black in the sun, with crows overhead and the ubiquitous gulls wheeling and twisting in the sky. Fish broke in the channel and kelp waved from the edges of half-submerged rocks, and the shores were so close and so silent that it seemed as if we had penetrated the heart of something. Not darkness, that was for sure, but a primeval presence that had never changed and would be everlasting. The rudderpost groaned in its bearings, the water hissed along the sides of the hull, a black crow cawed deep in the woods. A passenger reached for his camera.

"Don't bother," his companion said. "Something like this can't be captured on film."

"Fish broke in the channel and kelp waved from the edges of half-submerged rocks....The rudderpost groaned in its bearings, the water hissed along the sides of the hull, a black crow cawed deep in the woods."
The *Mercantile*.

V   *The Turn of the Tide*

Every age has its survivors which linger on after their contemporaries have gone.
                    —Robert Simper, *East Coast Sail*

We turned west at the top of Bartlett Island, threading our way below Newbury Neck and above Long Island, which dominates the upper half of Blue Hill Bay. Blue Hill itself— at 560 feet the major landmark on the peninsula bearing its name—was straight ahead. Viewed from where we were, broad-reaching with a rush of foam toward Blue Hill Harbor and the town of Blue Hill at its head, the primary colors were not at all blue but rather the dark green of the conifers and the light green of the hardwoods. The bluish cast of the hill, said to have been caused by great stands of blue spruce on its sides, has not been in evidence for the many decades since the old-growth forest was stripped away.

As the skipper brought us into the outer reaches of Blue Hill Harbor, one of the prettiest on the coast, a good part of the local yacht-club fleet—Blue Hill has a sizable summer community—was getting underway en masse for an afternoon race. A schooner in the middle of a racecourse is not unlike the proverbial bull in a china shop.

"Kollegewidgwok Yacht Club!" the skipper harrumphed, spinning the wheel and bringing the schooner through the eye of the wind onto the other tack. "Sounds like a German university for Chinese-Indians."

Like most of those who make their living from the sea on schooners, tugboats, fishing craft, freighters, and tankers, the skipper was contemptuous of yachts and yacht clubs and yachtsmen. His attitude was a reflection of the division between those who work with their hands and those who don't, or between "real sailors and idlers," as the skipper would put it more bluntly. It was also a legacy of that time, fifty to seventy-five years ago, when the cargo trade was dying and schoonermen found themselves without work. Most went off in other directions—motor vessels and fishing boats, perhaps—and the real old-timers retired. A few went into what is now known as the service sector—they became paid hands on private yachts and professional boatmen at yacht clubs, employed by summer people. It was quite a comedown for skippers and mates of coasting schooners, who had been proud of their independence. The lucky sailors who managed to hang on to berths in the

Flags and pennants flying, water casks along the lee rail, yawlboat snug in the davits, the *Stephen Taber* romps happily along on a reach.

few schooners still in operation looked down their noses at their former companions, thinking them damned fools who worked for damned-fool "rusticators" and "summer complaints."

Our skipper's attitude was paradoxical. His living had depended for years on the summer people, since most paying passengers in the schooner fleet were "from away," the polite down-east term for out-of-staters. (Impolite terms come and go, depending on the character of the visitors. "Straps" or "strap-hangers"—slang for subway riders—were hot for a while. Over in Camden, tourists are known as "cone-eaters," as so many of them buy ice-cream cones and eat them while strolling around the village. The locals presumably eat their ice cream in dishes, in the privacy of their own homes.)

But in the skipper's mind, he was still involved in the cargo-schooner tradition, since he was, in a way, carrying cargo—animate passengers instead of inanimate stone or lumber—and was not bowing and scraping to a bunch of yachtsmen in Breton red trousers and white boat shoes. (On his feet the skipper wore bright blue running shoes with the name of the manufacturer in oversize white lettering on the sides. "I don't run or jog, and I don't look like a damned-fool yachtsman either," he said.)

* * *

The Maine windjammer trade began in the 1930s as the last of the cargo coasters were seeing their final days. It was the heart of the Great Depression, which hit Maine particularly hard, and all sectors of the economy—the farms, the sawmills, the canneries, the shipyards, the boatshops, the shoe factories—were having a difficult time surviving. Little commerce meant few cargoes, and when that condition was coupled with the ever-increasing competition of trucks and railroads, the demise of the coasting schooner was ensured. At the beginning of the decade, for example, there were fewer than 100 small schooners still working the New England coast. By World War II, all but a handful were gone. They went so fast that the coast was just about empty of working sailing craft before anyone noticed that a way of life was threatened—not that anyone other than the sailors affected by the vessels' passing really gave a damn.

What happened to all those schooners over the years? Many were converted to power, their masts pulled or sawed off at the deck, pilothouses built on the afterdeck. They became freighters, sardine carriers, fishing draggers, and general-purpose lighters. Others had their rigs cut down and were used as barges hauled around the coasts by tugboats. Those that weren't so lucky were laid up in back coves and alongside derelict wharves in the hope that business would improve at a future date; they were taken to the breakers' yards to be stripped of salvageable gear and then broken up; they were driven ashore and burned where they lay. Quite a few were converted to other purposes. Some of those purposes were bizarre.

The three-masted stone schooner *Annie B. Mitchell* became a lobster storage pound. The *William Bisbee* was done over as a pirate ship for the Florida tourist trade. The *C.H. Edwards* was given a two-story house on her main deck and became a machine shop on

the Portland waterfront. The *Lavolta* was disguised as the *Arbella*, the ship that brought over the founders of the Massachusetts Bay Colony, and became the centerpiece for a tercentenary celebration. The *Fannie F. Hall* was transformed into the *Mayflower* of Plymouth, in the manner of a dress rehearsal for the full-scale replica built in England in the 1950s for that port. The *Regina* was hauled ashore to be set up on blocks; she became author Booth Tarkington's workshop and private museum in Kennebunkport. The *M.M. Hamilton*, a schooner that had been converted from the last of the Chebeague stone sloops,

Blue Hill Harbor. Blue Hill itself is in the right background. The faint outline of the Camden Hills, on the far side of Penobscot Bay, can be seen on the horizon.

was brought to Duxbury, Massachusetts, and turned into a laboratory for scientific research into marine borers. The *James L. Maloy* was transformed into a tearoom in Onset, Massachusetts. The list goes on and on. All of these vessels were given the short-term treatment: hard use, no maintenance, zero respect.

It was a sad era for the coasting schooners, as it was for their sisters that had served as fishermen and pilotboats. The vessels were disappearing so fast or being bowdlerized so thoroughly that in 1936 the federal government, through the Works Progress Administration, set up the Historic American Merchant Marine Survey, a special program to document as many as possible before they were gone completely (or, as it turned out, until the WPA ran out of money). It was obvious to anyone who took even a cursory look at the situation that in a decade or two at the outside, unless someone came up with a creative plan for its salvation, the schooner fleet would be merely a memory.

❋

Someone did come along—a fellow named Frank Swift, who in the mid-1930s was living with his wife in a camp he had built on Toddy Pond in East Orland, Maine. The Depression was in full swing. Swift may not have been as bad off as the hoboes riding the rails and the urban unemployed selling apples and pencils on the street and the itinerant farm workers scrabbling for oranges to pick and weeds to hoe, but he was living the marginal existence common in Maine during the Depression, making jewelry to sell to the tourists and trying a little of this and a little of that to make ends meet.

The notion of having a career—going to work at a job with a future—was alien to most Maine residents of the time, especially those living in the rural areas and on the down-east coast. Getting by—grabbing every meager, short-term opportunity that presented itself—was the rule rather than the exception. Digging clams, felling trees, raking blue-berries, packing sardines, selling gifts and antiques to the tourists—whatever it took to keep heat in the house and food on the table.

"I had to find something to provide for my family," Swift was to say later. "I had seen pulpwood vessels unloading in Bucksport, and I wondered why I couldn't get a vessel and instead of carrying freight, carry people on Maine-coast cruises." It was an interesting concept, though not totally original. Ever since summer people started coming to Maine, the locals have been entertaining them on the water in one fashion or another.

Nobody knows when the first Maine-coast fisherman took the first visitor out in his dory or sloopboat, but by the beginning of the twentieth century, there were plenty of coastal towns—Bar Harbor, Boothbay Harbor, Rockland, Portland, and others—where you could hire a boat and a skipper for yourself or join other passengers on a daysail. Many of the big hotels, like the Samoset in Rockland, had arrangements with owners of Friendship sloops and other types of traditional working craft, who would entertain vacationers with cruises on the bays, picnics on the islands, and fishing expeditions on the cod and haddock grounds. In the 1890s, for example, the ancient pinky *Susan*, built in Essex, Massachusetts, in 1820, was available in South Bristol to rusticators looking for the "authenticity" of the Maine way of living. For the modest price of admission, they got a chance to see the coast through the eyes of a working waterman and hear stories—often shamelessly embellished and therefore all the more amusing—in a dialect that was altogether charming to the ears of someone from Philadelphia, New York, or Boston.

✪

Frank Swift had experience at sea, but not in the coasting-schooner fleet. He was born in 1902 in Saranac Lake, New York, an Adirondack town with its own tradition of catering to summer residents and tourists. But Swift had a saltwater frame of mind, acquired in part from studying the contents of a sea chest that had belonged to his great-uncle, a harpooner on a whaling ship in the 1840s. With typical boyhood visions of exotic ports and fast sailing in the trade winds, he enrolled as a cadet aboard the schoolship *Newport*, a former U.S. Navy barkentine that served as New York state's floating merchant-marine academy. Subsequently he served as an able-bodied seaman, then quartermaster, aboard the Barber Line's steamship *Elkton*, which carried case oil to Hong Kong, Hawaii, and the Philippines.

The sea may have been in his blood, but Frank Swift had an artistic bent as well. In 1918–19, he studied silversmithing and jewelrymaking at a craft school in Milton, New York, and afterward took a job at the Val-Kil Forge in Hyde Park, New York, where he crafted pewter reproductions and jewelry. In the 1920s, he directed plays at a community theater in Poughkeepsie, New York, and in the summers worked as a counselor at a boys' camp in South Waterford, Maine, where he taught stagecraft. Eventually he moved to Maine permanently.

The genesis of Frank Swift's idea to take passengers on windjammer cruises came from his experiences as a summer-camp counselor. Occasionally the boys would go on field trips, and one of their favorites was a few days under sail on the coast aboard the schooner *George Cress*, skippered by Captain Parker Hall of Sandy Point, just below Bucksport at the mouth of the Penobscot River. The *Cress*, originally named the *Peter Mehrhof*, was a heavily built 79-foot Hudson River brick schooner of 1885. According to legend, she was renamed after a South Street (New York City) crimp—a broker who specialized in procuring seamen, willing or otherwise, for the coasting-schooner fleet. (Crimps were among the darker elements of the shipping business and were notorious for operating just shy of the antislavery laws. They would get sailors in hock and then sell their services to shipowners looking for a crew; get sailors drunk, haul them, still inebriated, aboard ship, depart with their advance wages, and take a promissory note for the rest; and, generally speaking, prey unmercifully on those who were down and out on the waterfront.)

In short, the *George Cress* was a salty old vessel with a colorful history, typical of the remaining small schooners still tramping along the coast during the last days of commercial sail. The camp boys and their counselors loved the carefree life on board, kicking around the coast. Here was a vessel that, unlike a yacht, didn't have to be coddled and polished and treated like a sacred icon. The boys brought their own bedding, just like

the real coastermen, drank water out of a cask, dove into the cold waters of the bay from the bowsprit and off the taffrail, and fished and skylarked and listened to the wild yarns of Captain Parker. They had a grand old time.

Captain Parker J. Hall was at the time the most famous skipper on the Maine coast, equal in fame in all of New England to Captain Zeb Tilton of Martha's Vineyard. Originally from Massachusetts, Captain Hall was born, it was thought, during the Civil War. (Some obituaries listed his age as eighty-six when he died in 1948—which, if true, would put his birthdate in 1862.) He came to Maine when he was middle-aged and was known far and wide as the "Lone Mariner of the New England Coast," since he preferred to sail without a crew—even though the normal complement on a vessel the size of the *George Cress* would have been two or three. (He took to sailing singlehanded early in his career after he had been attacked and robbed by his crew.) A stutterer, Captain Hall was a tough old buzzard who could do the work of five normal men and was as proficient at seamanship and seat-of-the-pants navigation as anyone who had ever stood behind the wheel of a schooner.

"He was a rugged individualist," wrote John Leavitt, "who liked to violate every ancient superstition of the seafaring profession. Blue paint he used in profusion, hatch covers flipped over on their backs, and he whistled, stuck knives in masts, and otherwise flouted seagoing convention with complete abandon. I asked him once how he managed to set a mainsail on those larger schooners with no hoisting engine and he replied, 'C-c-c-cal'late I w-w-w-was j-j-jest a m-m-m-mite hef-hef-heftier than th' m-m-mains'l.' He must have been nearing sixty or more at the time but he had the strength and agility of a much younger man. He was not tall, perhaps 5 feet 8 inches or even a little less, but he was so wide shouldered that he almost had to turn sideways to go through an average door, and he always did so going down a companionway. He probably weighed well over 200 pounds but it was mostly bone and muscle."

After Frank Swift left the boys' camp, he remained friends with Captain Hall, and in the mid-1930s, when Swift was struck by the inspiration to organize passenger cruises aboard coasting schooners, he went over to Sandy Point and discussed the idea with the captain. Did it not make sense? There were all those schooners, laid up and wasting away, and all those city folk just dying to get away from it all and savor a taste of the real Maine, and all those skippers, hands, and cooks on the beach without jobs. Wouldn't it work?

You would expect a man who had spent his entire life sailing boxboards out of Bangor and paving stone out of Vinalhaven to snicker and laugh over the idea of trading traditional coasting-schooner cargo for a bunch of rusticating secretaries and life-insurance salesmen. There is no way to tell what would have become of Frank Swift's idea if he had. But Captain Hall was no dope. He was well aware that if something wasn't done to put the remaining schooners to use, they would soon enough be gone.

Not to say that either man was approaching the matter with totally altruistic motives. Captain Parker Hall may have been a great seaman, but he was also a successful businessman. Frank Swift wasn't out to save the world; he was simply trying to keep his family's life together in a time of economic hardship. Perhaps this was a scheme that would put idle schooners and sailors to work, but above all, it was one that might provide a decent income and then some. Hall told Swift that this was a scheme that could make money; in fact, Hall was so enthusiastic he helped Swift locate a schooner and a skipper amenable to the endeavor. The latter requirement may not seem so important, but if a skipper resented summer people and tourists—and many of the old-timers did—such an attitude would work against the success of the operation. Then, as now, the personality of the skipper was as important as the condition of the vessel.

We worked our way back down Blue Hill Bay into the rising southwesterly breeze. Not as strong as it had been the day before, it was still enough to make tacking considerably easier than it would have been if the winds were light. Our schooner, like most built on the coasting-schooner model, was what is known to sailors as slow in stays. She would respond very slowly to the rudder when we tacked unless there was considerable pressure on her sails from the wind. To counteract this tendency, just before we would tack, the skipper would bear off slightly to make sure the sails were full and gain all the speed he could, then boom down the deck, "Ready about!" and the mate, assisted by a few passengers, would stand by the jibsheets. The skipper would then announce, "Hard alee!" and throw the helm down quickly, spinning the spokes of the wheel in long strokes like a barker at a carnival spinning the Wheel of Fortune.

The schooner would slowly—ponderously it seemed at critical times—pivot on the centerboard, the bowsprit describing an arc on the horizon, the stern swinging a similar arc aft. As the bow came up into the wind, the sails shuddering and shaking in the breeze, the mate's gang would cast off the jibsheet; then, as the bow kept swinging over onto the new tack, they would trim in the other sheet of the jib and, when the skipper nodded that it was trimmed right, secure it. The mate and his party would then trim the staysail sheet if necessary and work their way to the foresail and main.

Should the vessel resist falling off onto the other tack, the mate would not cast off the jibsheet after the bow passed the eye of the wind. The jib would therefore be backed—restrained on the "wrong" side—and the pressure of the wind on it would force the bow over. In some circumstances—such as when the direction of the seas might make tacking especially difficult—the mate might back the staysail as well to give the bow an extra jolt of wind.

There are those times, thankfully rare, when Murphy's Law takes over and everything seems to conspire against tacking properly. The vessel might "miss stays"—come up toward the eye of the wind, hesitate, and fall right back onto the original tack—or come up into the wind and become locked there "in irons," the sails shimmying and the sheets slashing back and forth. In the latter situation, quickly backing the headsails will bring her around, but in the former, the only recourse is to build up speed and try again. (In an emergency, if the vessel has an auxiliary engine or if the yawlboat is rigged

and ready to go, the skipper can drive her around with power.)

Missing stays is not a big deal out in the open water with no other vessels around and plenty of room to maneuver, but it's serious business in confined quarters. A passenger schooner once missed stays on an ebbing tide at the mouth of Pulpit Harbor as she was trying to clear Pulpit Rock. She was forced down on the ledge, where she remained pinned as the tide went out, leaving her high and dry. They got her off later without much damage, but the embarrassment to the skipper and crew as they sat on the ledge waiting for the next high tide to float their schooner free was acute, to say the least.

But tacking ship and missing stays and trimming sheets were of concern only to the crew and the handful of guests who cared about the working of our schooner. Most of the passengers were along for the beautiful vistas and the penetrating warmth of the sun, and they were getting plenty of both—hills, headlands, islands, mountains, half-tide ledges with foaming green-blue waves surging around them, lobsterboats, the occasional pleasure boat. As we reached the lower end of the bay, a schooner emerged from Casco Passage, a long pennant streaming from her main topmast and an American flag at the leech of her mainsail.

"That's the *Isaac H. Evans*, Captain Eddie Glaser, out of Rockland, Maine, the U.S. of A., bound for everyplace," the skipper said, taking off his cap and waving it. A puff of smoke mushroomed over the side of the *Evans* and trailed off astern. A few seconds later, the report of her saluting cannon whacked the side of our hull. It was a little brass breech-loading swivel mounted on her starboard rail. "Damn," the skipper said. "Someday I've got to get one of those things."

One of the passengers pointed out that the *Evans* over there and our schooner over here were living museums of maritime history.

"It's better than that," the skipper said. "These schooners are alive because they work just like in the old days. Museums can't keep schooners in stock because they're dead. They're quickly gone. Museums are death to wooden schooners."

Though characteristically bluntly stated, there was a certain validity to the skipper's view. Following the death of commercial cargo-carrying sail, scores of established museums, and museums specially established for the purpose, acquired vessels and put them on exhibit. A few were hauled out on land, where they baked in the sun and their planks shrank and their seams opened and rainwater worked its devious way into every crevice. The rot and decay progressed exponentially. Most vessels were left in the water, moored next to a wharf or quay, and, though the deterioration was slower, it nevertheless took place.

Just as an unheated, unoccupied, unused house will quickly fall to rack and ruin, an idle wooden ship will deteriorate faster than she would if sailed, despite the best intentions of the institution in charge of her well-being. Though it is true that a full-time shipkeeping crew will be able to minimize the decay considerably—witness the U.S. Navy's success with the USS *Constitution*, "Old Ironsides," in Charlestown, Massachusetts—most museums do not have the resources to provide such a crew.

The *Isaac H. Evans* at anchor in a calm. An awning is rigged under her forward boom, and the yawlboat has come alongside the boarding ladder to take passengers ashore.

"More schooners have survived as working vessels than as museum exhibits," the skipper said, "and that's a fact."

Consider, for example, the schooner *Bowdoin*, one of the current stalwarts of the Maine coast. Launched in 1921 at the Hodgdon Brothers yard in East Boothbay, she was heavily planked and framed of the very best white oak to withstand the worst conditions of the northern seas, as she was designed on a fishing-schooner model specifically for Arctic exploration. Under the capable hands of her owner, Admiral Donald B. MacMillan, she proved her superiority in twenty-six voyages and almost 300,000 miles in some of the most hostile waters of the world, surviving innumerable gales, brushes with ice, and groundings.

In 1959, his career ended, MacMillan donated the *Bowdoin* to the Mystic Seaport Museum in Connecticut. The vessel was in remarkably good condition at the time, considering her experiences, and MacMillan expected she would stay that way. Eight years later, she was a mess. The museum's priority at the time was the development of its site, not the care of its vessels, and the *Bowdoin* went downhill rapidly in the absence of even routine maintenance. She deteriorated so quickly, in fact, that she was taken out of exhibition and laid up, which made matters worse. Covered with a plastic tarp, she became a greenhouse for rot.

Admiral MacMillan, to put it mildly, was exercised. He encouraged the formation of an association to take over the schooner from the museum and bring her back to Maine. After years of hard work and herculean fund-raising efforts, the Schooner Bowdoin Association managed to return her to sailing condition. Some of those who contributed to her renaissance were passenger schoonermen Captain Jim Sharp, formerly of the *Adventure*, and Captain John Nugent of the day schooner *Olad* out of Camden, and boatbuilder Jim Stevens of the venerable Goudy & Stevens shipyard, located next to the yard where the *Bowdoin* was originally built. Today, operated by the cadets at the Maine Maritime Academy in Castine, the *Bowdoin* lives because she is used.

✶

Frank Swift's first season in the passenger-schooner trade was the summer of 1936. Even though there was a rather large supply of schooners on the market that year, because the demand—and therefore the asking price of a fully found vessel—was low and getting lower, Swift couldn't afford to buy a schooner outright. Actually, even if he could have, Captain Parker Hall had suggested that Swift test the waters modestly, rather than rush into an innovative business that might prove to be a poor investment. The ideal situation, Captain Hall thought, was to charter a schooner for a single season. The capital outlay would be minimal, and Swift would be better able to find a vessel that was still in working condition, one that hadn't been laid up for a long period and therefore would not need more upgrading than a single season demanded.

Swift found what he was looking for in the centerboarder *Mabel*, at 54 feet and 37 tons one of the smaller schooners on the Maine coast—and for that reason the perfect vessel for a new venture into unknown territory. Built in 1881 in Milbridge, Maine, she had seen

Admiral Donald MacMillan's old arctic schooner *Bowdoin* underway in Eggemoggin Reach. Launched in 1921 in East Boothbay, retired in 1959 to become a museum ship, she was later restored to sailing condition and now is a training vessel for the Maine Maritime Academy in Castine.

thousands of tons of cargo—bricks, cordwood, hay, coal, lumber—pass through her hatches, but she was in remarkably good structural condition and was available for the season. It wasn't much of a job to clear her hold and build rudimentary cabins for eight passengers, and to rig her properly as a sailing vessel. Captain William Shepard, one of the veteran coastermen of Deer Isle, was signed on as skipper, his wife was hired as cook, and the *Mabel* was brought to Camden on the western shore of Penobscot Bay for a season of sailing.

The vessel and the skipper and the cook may have been right, but the year, 1936, was wrong. The health of the economy had improved slightly since the onslaught of the Depression, but vacationers and tourists were still scarce, and Swift was competing with hotels, guest houses, fishing camps, and cabins in the pines—all with established reputations and all with rock-bottom prices. Even at $25 per passenger, meals included, for a week-long cruise, Frank Swift had difficulty persuading people to try this barebones way of seeing the bay and the islands. No track record, no money to spend on advertising, lots of wrinkles to be ironed out.

"We had only three lady passengers on our first trip," Swift was to say later. "The next time, I believe, we took off without any passengers."

By the end of that first, short season, the best you could say was that Swift had gained experience and a sense of what would work and what would not. Come the end of the summer, he went back to Toddy Pond, Captain Shepard and his wife returned to Deer Isle, and the *Mabel* went back to her owner. In short order she was sold to a down-east fish-packing company as a sardine freighter; her accommodations were torn out, her rig was cut down, and an engine was installed.

But the *Mabel*, it seems, was destined for the windjammer trade. Shortly after World War II, when Frank Swift's Windjammer Cruises, as he called his business, finally came into its own, the little freighter was offered for sale again. Swift purchased her this time, rather than chartering her, rerigged her as a schooner, and put her back to work in the passenger trade, where she lasted until the late 1950s.

Slow, disappointing start or not, Frank Swift had been undeterred. In 1937 he chartered the *Lydia M. Webster*, a 58-footer built in Castine in 1882—a capable but homely little schooner with a nearly straight stem and a flattened sheer. The latter characteristic is a sure sign of a tired-out wooden vessel, and sure enough, after Swift bought her outright and drove her hard for a few seasons, she became too difficult to maintain and was dropped from the fleet.

That second year hadn't been much better than the first, and it appeared that there wasn't much future for this type of business, at least not the way it had been run to date. The *Webster*, like the *Mabel*, didn't have much capacity, but that didn't matter, as a week with only five passengers was considered a great accomplishment. What to do? Pack it in? Limp along marginally, depending on word-of-mouth advertising? Up the ante and go for broke?

Captain Swift—which is what he had become by then, an experienced skipper—

decided to give it one last shot, pull out all the stops, recharter the *Lydia M. Webster*, buy another schooner, advertise, and raise his prices to pay for it all. (To raise your prices in 1938, when a dollar was still a dollar, meant jumping from the 1927 $27-per-person rate to $30 for one week and offering a $10 discount for two weeks.) Strapped for cash, however, he couldn't afford even the few hundred dollars then asked for a seaworthy schooner. On the advice of Captain Hall, he therefore bought the *Annie F. Kimball*, which was laid up at Great Wass Island and in need of serious work to make her serviceable. In fact, she had to be considerably recaulked on Great Wass before she could even be sailed to Sandy Point to be grounded out on the beach for conversion. There, Swift hired a gang of unemployed carpenters and shipwrights.

"It required several days to overhaul the rigging, partly install cabins for ten passengers, and paint her," Captain Swift said later. "It was fortunate that I had good credit at the lumberyards and food stores in Camden, Belfast, and Rockland, because I was still operating on a shoestring." It was also fortunate that those businesses saw fit to extend credit, because in future years, when windjamming took off, they would gain considerable trade from a grateful skipper.

The *Annie F. Kimball*, like the *Mabel* and the *Lydia M. Webster*, was small and old (56 feet long, built in 1886 in Boothbay), but she was a pretty little thing that quickly came to be known as the "Pride of the Penobscot." A bay coaster with many characteristics of a fishing schooner, she had been a Maine coast regular, homeported during her cargo-carrying days variously in Deer Isle, Boothbay, and Jonesport.

With the *Webster* and the *Kimball*, Captain Frank Swift finally hit upon the formula for success: Advertise, stick it out through thick and thin, offer potential passengers a choice of schooners, buy cheap, don't get fancy, keep maintenance expenses down to the bare bones, and—most of all—don't be sentimental. If a schooner can't hack it, toss her aside and get another. In the twenty-five years Captain Swift remained in the passenger trade, he owned or chartered twelve different vessels, including several Maine coasting schooners, one from the Chesapeake, a yacht, and even Captain Irving Johnson's famous *Yankee*, a former North Sea pilotboat.

But all of Captain Swift's passenger schooners didn't get thrown away. When Swift retired in 1961, he sold two of them, the *Mattie* and the *Mercantile*, to Jim Nisbet, who later sold them to Les Bex, who sold them to Ray Williamson. They remain to this day in the Maine windjammer fleet. (In 1990, after a complete rebuild, the *Mattie* reverted to her original name, the *Grace Bailey*.) Affectionately known as the "green boats" because of their traditional dark-green topsides, they sail out of Camden, following the same routes as their sisters back in the 1930s.

❋

Late afternoon found us in the lowest reaches of Blue Hill Bay—the northern neck of Swans Island on one side and Bass Harbor, at the southern end of Mount Desert, on the other. We had such a good sailing breeze that the skipper, rather than take us into

Mackerel Cove or Bass Harbor for the night, kept us straight on through the passage between Placentia and Swans, down for a tantalizing peek into Lunt Harbor and the tiny village of Frenchboro ("How do you like that for an island community?" the skipper said, pointing past the anchored lobsterboats to the white church, the white school, the white houses connected by beaten paths), over toward Great Duck, and then north to the Western Way, which leads past the Cranberry Isles into Southwest Harbor.

The mountains of Mount Desert, the centerpieces of Acadia National Park, stood proud against the purple sky. Gray-and-white gulls wheeled around fishing boats making their way back to harbor. A black-hulled Coast Guard buoy tender, overhauling a channel buoy, heaved in the swell rolling up from the Gulf of Maine. The coasties, usually a jaded sort accustomed to a daylong variety of interesting watercraft, nevertheless lined the rail to watch us sweep past. An officer on the bridge cupped his hands to his mouth. "You're the fifth in an hour," he yelled, "but you're the best!"

"The best?" the skipper said under his breath, doffing his cap like Prince Philip acknowledging the cheers of the commoners. "You bet your boots we're the best. This is the finest schooner on the coast of Maine and...Hell's bells!...Mate!...Whip that foredeck crowd into shape. We're going to jibe. Right now. Let's go."

Up ahead in Southwest Harbor was the usual complement of visiting and local yachts, lobsterboats, and other craft, plus four schooners: the white-hulled *Timberwind*, the black-hulled *J. & E. Riggin*, the brightly painted *Heritage*, and the private schooner-yacht *Deliverance*. Their heavy masts and delicate rigging were silhouetted against a luminist's sky.

"No room for us," the skipper said. "They've got all the good holding ground. Someone ask the cook to come up here and call the harbormaster over to Northeast Harbor on the radio. If it's clear, we'll go in there." The answer, as it turned out, was yes, all clear.

The wind, right on our stern, died with the sun. We drifted with the incoming tide and not even a hint of a breeze up the channel toward the inner harbor, the skipper a study of outward calm, his inner tension betrayed only by the occasional twitching of his jaw muscles. It was a straight shot with an audience. Several people stood, cocktails in hand, on the balconies of their summer "cottages"—huge, old-money estates—watching the sunset, pink and orange, illuminate our sails. Nobody spoke. It was so silent we thought we could hear the clink of the ice in the cottagers' glasses.

We drifted on and on and on and on, an eighth of a mile, a quarter of a mile, the sails hanging in limp folds from the gaffs, the mate standing by the foredeck winch, waiting to let the anchor go. Finally, after the skipper had wrung the last ounce of forward momentum out of the schooner, when it seemed as if time had stopped and the entire universe was vibrating like a tuning fork, he nodded to the mate. The anchor splashed into the water. The chain roared through the hawsepipe. The sounds echoed off the hills and the cottages, then died away. We were attached by a silver thread to the deep, black pool of Northeast Harbor.

Three schooners, at the
end of a perfect day of
sailing, make their way
with the last of the breeze
toward a snug anchorage.

VI *Fog Mulls and Black Pigs*

In that sense of direct inheritance, the few venerable coasters among today's windjammers, from wherever they were launched, are the legitimate heirs to Maine's carefully nurtured but still credible tradition of pokin' 'long, pickin' up th' buoys in th' dam thick, mebbe nosin' up Tenants way with th' toyde, when an' if it scayles up, fer thet lot o' ax han'les Fred promised an' a deck-lud o' hay, eff th' gol ram sun'll jes' peek aout long 'nuff t' droy th' fethahs on a shag.

— Joseph E. Garland, *Adventure, Queen of the Windjammers*

There's no other way to describe it. Wednesday morning came weird. Mist on the water, clouds pushing in from the west, atmosphere with a clammy moistness that demanded a woolen sweater. As soon as you put one on, you felt hot and steamy.

"Weather change coming on," the skipper said, tuning in to the NOAA mariner's advisory.

"…Matinicus Rock, wind south-southeast, 4 knots." The weathercaster sounded like a drunk gargling through a mouthful of mothballs. "Mount Desert Rock, south at 6. Cashes Ledge Buoy, south at 6 knots, air temperature 57, sea temperature 59, three-foot seas every nine seconds. Variable cloudiness with patches of fog reported all along the coast. Visibility six to eight miles, under one mile in fog. Rockland has a southeast wind at 2 knots, Southwest Harbor calm wind, Jonesport south-southeast 3 knots. Now for the mariner's weather discussion…."

"Hold on to your hats," the skipper said, wincing.

"A tropical storm, currently off the Carolinas, is working its way up the eastern seaboard and is expected to veer off to the eastward at Cape Cod. High winds, high seas, higher than normal tides, and heavy rain are expected later tonight and into tomorrow from Massachusetts northeastward to the Bay of Fundy and Nova Scotia…."

Following breakfast—a knock-down-drag-out affair of pancakes with more blueberries than batter, country-sausage patties the diameter of coffee-can covers, and maple syrup that tasted pure and very well could have been—the skipper announced his plan to the assembled ship's company.

"I figure we'll have an interesting day of sailing before the weather gets nasty," he said. "Anyone who wants supplies for the next day or so better go into town with the yawlboat, because tonight this schooner's going to be buttoned down tighter than a hermit crab in a borrowed shell. You want beer, toothpaste, shoelaces, get it now."

A boatload of passengers and crew return to the *Adventure* after a trip to town for supplies. Anyone who wants to gets a turn at the oars.

So a boatload of passengers went ashore while the skipper pored over his charts and considered the alternatives. He had a lot of alternatives to consider, but in the age-old tradition of command at sea, he kept his deliberations for the most part to himself. He had a few words with the mate and talked for a bit over the radiotelephone with the skipper of the *Timberwind*, which was over in Southwest Harbor, and the *Mercantile*, which was in Bucks Harbor, made a few notes in his pocket notebook, and then dropped down into the yawlboat lying to her painter under the schooner's transom. He checked over the engine carefully and made sure there was an ample supply of fuel in the tank.

We got underway at 9:30 in the morning. The wind was moderate and blowing into the harbor, so we pushed out with the yawlboat, leisurely raising the working sails in the long, lazy swell off Bear Island, then taking the Eastern Way past Sutton Island and Little Cranberry Island. It was a calm and relaxing sail, all smiles and handshakes, until suddenly behind us, coming up fast in our wake, was the *Heritage*, one of the newest and finest schooners in the fleet. She was a smart sailer, made all the smarter by a press of canvas that included a topsail and a flying jib. Her skipper, Captain Douglas Lee, was so proud of his vessel that he never missed an opportunity to show her off.

"Bloody blast it all to hell!" our skipper said, caught by surprise. Our yawlboat was still astern, slowing us down, and the topsails were still in their stops.

"Too late to make it a race," the mate moaned. "Lee has got us now."

Our skipper and Captain Lee were great rivals, always ready to duke it out whenever the opportunity arose. In a matter of seconds, the *Heritage* came storming up to our stern, hung there for a tantalizing moment, then pulled out and surged along our windward side, blanketing our sails and slowing us down even further. The gap between the two schooners couldn't have been more than fifty feet. Passengers crowded the rail of the *Heritage*. Her mate, halfway up the main shrouds, was grinning like the Cheshire cat. Her skipper, in the nonchalant pose affected by all schooner captains in the presence of an audience— especially one that has been thoroughly whipped—was chomping on a fat cigar.

"Good morning, Captain," Captain Lee said cheerfully in a singsong voice at the exact moment when the two schooners were precisely aligned, windlass to windlass, deckhouse to deckhouse, mainmast to mainmast, wheel to wheel, skipper to skipper. "Your vessel sure makes a handsome sight this morning." Our skipper tipped his cap politely.

"Say, mate," Captain Lee called out. "See if you can do something to slow this schooner down. We seem to be going too fast."

Our skipper's face turned to stone. "Nuts," he said under his breath, not even moving his lips while he said it. Without a sideways peek at the *Heritage*, he leaned over the chart on the top of the cabinhouse and pretended to check a distance with a pair of brass navigational dividers. Our mate leaned over to tie his shoes, showing his backside to the other schooner.

It was over in a matter of minutes ("Thanks be to God," the mate whispered). The *Heritage* pulled ahead, cut across our bow, jibed her sails over, and shot under our lee back into the Eastern Way. Meanwhile, we hauled the yawlboat up into the stern davits and

"Suddenly behind us, coming
up fast in our wake, was the
Heritage....She was a smart
sailer, made all the smarter
by a press of canvas that included a topsail and a flying
jib."

set the topsails while the skipper, after calling angrily to the cook for a cup of coffee, vowed revenge at the earliest possible moment.

✹

By midmorning we were drifting among the islands off the southern end of Mount Desert in a flat, oily ocean and a cloud cover like the gray underside of a low steel roof. Pink granite, dismal green spruce, the surface of the sea the color of cast iron. The water was ruffled here and there by stray breezes first from the southeast, then from the east, then from the south, then from the north—a confusion of directions that made the sails slat back and forth randomly; the booms and gaffs, brought up short by the rigging, jolted the schooner as if she were being slapped by a giant hand. Every once in a while, we would pick up one of the puffs and, after much running around and adjusting of sheets by the deck gang, would surge along for a few hundred yards until the breeze was gone and the sails and the sheets would go limp again.

We weren't alone on the heaving sea, though there was an indefinable loneliness to the scene, not unlike the isolation one can feel walking down a major boulevard in a strange city. We were here and everything else was there, and between us was a vast expanse of trackless space. Several schooners were in sight, a yacht or two, and a couple of sprit-rigged pulling boats, dirty white on the outside, orange-red on the inside, from the Hurricane Island Outward Bound School. And, of course, the usual complement of lobsterboats racing from trap buoy to trap buoy, the fishermen driving their craft as if they were at the wheel of Grand Prix race cars taking the turns at Monte Carlo. One of the boats, a cross between a traditional down east lobsterboat and a drug smuggler's switchblade, had a super-amplified stereo system aboard. No chanteys for this salt of the sea; not at all. Across the water came the disembodied voices of Pete Townshend and Roger Daltrey, "Whooo are you? Who-who? Who-who?...."

The skipper, still smarting from our encounter with the *Heritage*, was disgusted. "That...that...*thing* over there," he said, pointing with the soggy end of a half-smoked green cigar, "is a sorry excuse for a lobsterboat, and the jughead who's driving it is so brainless he probably cleans both ears with one continuous Q-tip."

To say that our skipper was an unreconstructed traditionalist would be putting it mildly. He, like many of his colleagues, believed in the timelessness of the sea and the enduring nature of the working vessels of the coast. He gave little thought to the changing fashions of the yachts and the pleasure craft—in fact, he expected such changes to take place and saw them as evidence of the corruptions of modern society—but he considered traditional vessels to be just that, and therefore was appalled by the introduction of modern devices, especially electronics, on schooners, lobsterboats, sardine carriers, fishing draggers, and the like. (Never mind that he loved his own radio.)

The changes on the coast of Maine since the last days of cargo-carrying and fishing under sail have been even greater than the skipper would have liked to admit. Just as there were still a few sailing coasters in the 1930s, there were also a handful of lobstermen who

"We would pick up one of the puffs and, after much running around and adjusting of sheets by the deck gang, would surge along for a few hundred yards until the breeze was gone and the sails and the sheets would go limp." The *Mary Day*.

place but over time drew closer and closer. Like an amorphous monster out of a science-fiction movie, it oozed to the westward and swallowed everything in its path. First a distant schooner, then several yachts, then another schooner, a lobsterboat and another and another, then the sea buoy off the southern end of Baker Island—all disappeared as if they had never existed— and then us. With the fog came a damp chill and a strange condition that muffled or silenced some sounds and amplified others. Lobsterboats that we knew were about a mile away sounded as if they were just beyond the range of our vision, which was maybe a hundred feet; the swell breaking on the shore of Baker Island, about half a mile away, sounded as if it were in a distant world, both miles away and high above the surface of the water. The loneliness of the day became lonelier.

"Ears are more valuable than your eyes in the fog," Roger Duncan wrote in *A Cruising Guide to the New England Coast*. "Fog seems to affect the transmission of sound. A horn clearly audible ten miles away may fade out at three miles and nearly blow you out of your shirt at half a mile."

"With the fog came a damp chill and a strange condition that muffled or silenced some sounds and amplified others." The *Sylvina W. Beal.*

Overall we could hear a cacophony of sounds made by fog signaling devices. The whistle on the buoy south of Baker Island, the canned-air horns of the lobsterboats and some of the yachts, and the whistles of the rest. The mate sent one of our passengers forward with an old-fashioned fisherman-style hand-cranked horn, which didn't so much blast as bleat like a lost sheep.

According to the rules of the nautical road, signals are required for all vessels underway in the fog—powered vessels must sound a prolonged blast every minute; sailboats, one long and two short blasts; all vessels at anchor, five seconds of bell-ringing per minute. In our vicinity, with lots of vessels nearby, the signals produced an avant-garde symphony in which one sound was virtually indistinguishable from the next—and, worse, the direction from which the sounds were coming was next to impossible to determine. Our crew, however, had considerable experience in the fog and was surprisingly calm in the face of it. They were quite skilled in figuring out what vessel out there was where and what direction it was taking. Which was a good thing, because we were right in the middle of what is known in the trade as a dungeon o' fog, the penultimate condition.

On the coast of Maine, the general term for fogginess is a "fog mull," but there are several grades of this, each with its own distinctive descriptive phrase. In ascending order of density, they are "a mite thick," "thick o' fog," "a dungeon o' fog," and "a thick dungeon o' fog." In "a dungeon o' fog," the helmsman on a medium-size vessel such as ours would not be able to see much beyond the bowsprit. In "a thick dungeon o' fog," heavy-duty stuff, the moisture is so dense as to make a visually impenetrable wall a few feet in front of your eyes.

"This is what I like about windjamming," the skipper said sarcastically, wiping the condensation from his glasses. "The view."

Aside from the danger of collision with other vessels, we were in a relatively good position, as the skipper had taken us on a course away from Mount Desert and there were no islands or ledges in our path. Yet the crew was taking no chances. The mate was keeping a lookout up in the bow, the cook was amidships on the starboard side, the galley mate was on the port side, and the passengers were instructed to keep their eyes peeled.

There are legendary stories along the coast about the old-timers and their uncanny abilities to find their way through the fog by seat-of-the-pants navigation. It is said that some could navigate by smell, sniffing out spruce trees on islands and headlands, mudflats, sawn oak in shipyards, lumber schooners with aromatic cargoes (especially cedar shingles), even canneries alongshore—each supposedly with its own odor. They could also navigate by listening to "the rote," the sound of the waves on the shore. On steep, sandy shores, it pounds. On open shores, with rounded rocks and boulders, it rolls and grinds. On sharp ledges and granite cliffs, it crashes. A sailor who was so familiar with the geological characteristics of the coast, who was as familiar with the trend of the shore as the winding of the path to the outhouse back home, would listen carefully and "make the rote."

And then there were the old-timers who studied the waterfowl. Giles M.S. Tod, in *The*

Last Days of Sail Down East, relates a wonderful story about Captain Zeb Tilton and the *Alice S. Wentworth*. Captain Zeb was sailing close to shore in a thick o' fog with a young boy up in the bow keeping a lookout.

"Suddenly the boy shouted aft that there were ducks ahead. The old man hollered forward: 'Be they walking or be they swimming?'

"When the boy called back that he thought they were walking, the captain yelled: 'All right, then, me lad, ready about and hard alee!' thus taking his vessel back into deeper waters."

✳

No sailor, however experienced, likes to spend extended periods in the fog, especially close in to a shore as island- and ledge-infested as that of Maine. But our skipper, after listening once again to the NOAA weather forecast, was confident we were in a large patch that would either slide back to whence it came or that we could sail out of in short order. And sure enough, after about an hour's worth of feeling our way on pins and needles, we broke through an edge into clear air. It was still cloudy and the winds were still as fluky as they had been in the morning, but we could see where we were going and where we had been. We were not very far from Little Duck Island.

If the forecast had been for all-out fogginess for an indefinite period, the skipper would have been faced with one of two choices: sail offshore until the fog cleared, or feel his way into a harbor, anchor, and wait out the weather. For a passenger schooner, the latter choice may not cause too many problems, but for the old cargo skippers, to be fogbound meant the loss of time and therefore money. To the crews, though, it could be a calm respite, a vacation from hard work.

"In a remote harbor or cove," wrote John Leavitt, "there is something even pleasant in this kind of fog. Perhaps not to the skipper chafing at the delay which prevents him from getting to his next loading or discharging port, although most of them had been too long on the coast to take it other than philosophically. There is nothing to do under such circumstances except eat and sleep, read or work on hobbies, and there is genuine peace and quietude, completely insulated from the rest of the world. How many times at the end of a period of frenzied business activity in the city in recent years have I wished I could be in one of my old bunks, waiting out a fog mull in some quiet down-east harbor!"

Such a cargo schooner may have been lucky enough to be biding its time in a coastal town—a place like Stonington or Carvers Harbor or Castine—where there were stores and, in some cases, an opera house for entertainment. (In Maine, an opera house was usually a multipurpose hall for vaudeville acts, movies, stereopticon shows, lectures, town meetings, plays, and even the occasional traveling opera show. Many towns, such as Camden, Stonington, Rockport, and Belfast, still have their old opera houses and use them regularly.) If not, perhaps there may have been a trader at anchor nearby.

Traders were schooners fitted out as floating stores. They carried everything landside general stores might stock, plus much they didn't. Homeported in larger towns such as

Rockland and Portland, they would sail downeast with an assorted cargo of canned and bulk goods, clothes, boots, foulweather gear, tools, fishing supplies, ax handles, tobacco, candy, pulp novels, kitchen utensils—anything and everything that might be in demand at the moment—and anchor for a week or so in harbors, coves, and, if possible, tidal rivers deep inland near isolated communities. Better still than anchoring, they would lie to a wharf if such were available, easily accessible to their customers. Word would go out to the farthest reaches of the countryside—"There's a trader down at the old mill wharf"— and people would come from far and near to stock up on supplies. The traders' heyday came before World War I, when a veritable fleet of them ranged the coast, but for several years afterward, a few still called at some of the island villages.

"As may be imagined," wrote George Wasson in *Sailing Days on the Penobscot*, "the local storekeeper was by no means enthusiastic over the visits of traders, and viewed them in much the same spirit often shown in later days towards department and chain stores.... The prime requisite for a trader was a wide, stiff vessel, not easily careened by wind. She must also be of shoal draft in order to lie at the smallest wharf in out-of-the-way 'gunkholes' where the best trade was found. On deck, between the masts, was built a diminutive but real house, clapboarded and shingled, with doors in the after end and windows upon one side. A sign prominently announced 'Five and Ten Cent Counter.' The foresail was cut high in order to swing over the house on deck.... These vessels were always well along in years and sometimes they were badly strained through long lying aground at wharves only suitable for smaller craft."

Perhaps the most colorful floating entrepreneur on the coast during the old days was a cobbler named Cottle, who built a flat-bottomed sailing scow—reputedly a slow, ungainly, unseaworthy craft—and sailed it from harbor to harbor. The scow had a rickety house built on deck with windows on the sides and a rusty stovepipe sticking up through the roof. A sign on the house read: W. Cottle. Boots and Shoes Repaired on the Rolling Deep. Cottle would blow into a seaside town or village on a fair wind, ground out his floating workshop on a beach or a mudflat, and stay there until he had repaired all the boots and shoes and harnesses there were to be repaired. Then, on the next fair wind and tide, he would be off to the next harbor.

Closely allied to the traders were the packets, schooners that followed regular routes along the coast, carrying passengers and freight. Forerunners of the steamboats that connected the down east ports to the major cities and towns to the westward, many of them continued on into the steamboat era, especially those that called on harbors never served by the steamers. They were the principal mode of transportation in and out of most of the small coastal and island communities of Maine. At the beginning of the Civil War, near the height of the packet trade, there were as many as twenty individual packet lines serving Maine from Boston.

Packets traveled on a set schedule—at least as set as any schedule could be that was subject to the vagaries of the wind and tide—and departed from their own wharves in Portland, Boothbay Harbor, Rockland, Bangor, and others. In Portland, for example, a

The *Mary Day* in a flat calm. It's time for her skipper to start thinking about whistling up a wind.

fleet of packets left from Widgery's Wharf, which was also known as the Portland Packet Pier.

Though today's windjammers carry passengers only, no freight, and concentrate on bringing them out and back from here to here, instead of from here to there, they are nevertheless a continuation of the packet tradition. In fact, many of the early windjammers of the Frank Swift fleet had been packets. The first schooner Captain Swift bought outright, the *Annie F. Kimball*, ran out of Southwest Harbor to ports to the eastward. Others included the *Lois M. Candage*, the *Lillian*, and the *Enterprise*, which had been specially built on Deer Isle for the packet trade and therefore was ideally suited for conversion to a cruise schooner.

✦

About one-thirty in the afternoon, the wind came up hard from the south-southeast, heeling the schooner over sharply and causing the mate and the galley hand to scramble into the rigging to furl the topsails and ease the pressure. We boiled along past Richs Head on Long Island, still sailing outside the islands, our course to the southwestward.

But the wind died as quickly as it rose, leaving us adrift in a scum of driftwood and floating seaweed and seabird feathers, sliding slowly along in a tidal current that was setting us in toward Marshall Island, the major island in the approaches to Jericho Bay. The sails slatted and slapped as the vessel rolled back and forth with the long, easy swell that was heaving in from the Gulf of Maine. The skipper, watching us slowly bearing down sideways toward Black Ledge, became apprehensive.

"Let's get the yawlboat down and start the engine," he said.

So the mate climbed into the yawlboat and we lowered away until he and the boat were out of sight under the transom. There was the sound of the starter, then nothing. Again, and again nothing. Then cursing, and nothing.

"Calling an engine a blankety-blank shithead won't get it started," the skipper yelled over the stern. "Come up here, mate, and take the wheel. I'll give it a try." We drifted closer to the ledge, which was populated by a couple of fat seals and half a dozen shags holding their wings outstretched as if welcoming our schooner into their embrace.

The skipper, an expert mechanic, struggled with the engine for a quarter of an hour until he pinpointed the problem: a dirty fuel-line filter. Every thirty seconds or so, he would look up at the ledge from the little engine compartment and say, "Holy bumblebee piss!" or some such thing, and dive back in again. Finally, after the shags and seals had cleared out for quieter territory, just when it seemed the schooner's side would be ground to hamburger on the jagged rock, the engine coughed and started. The yawlboat pushed us past Black Ledge and between Spirit and Drunkard ledges, and we were into the lower reaches of Jericho Bay.

The episode with the engine made the skipper jumpy and impatient. Here we were, windless, our old fog bank within sight to the east, the edge of a tropical storm, unseen and yet to be felt, to the southwest, a dull sky above and a greenish-black sea below. The passengers were bored and listless, the cook was down below arguing with the galley assistant....

"We need wind!" the skipper bellowed at the sails.

There are various ways to raise a breeze, all of them quite dangerous, as there is no way to control the size of the breeze once you have called for it. You can call a breeze and get a zephyr, or call a breeze and get a hurricane. There's just no way to tell in advance what you are going to get. Some sailors, however, think there is. They think there is a sliding scale of severity, starting with sticking a knife into the mast to raise a quiet breeze, next throwing a penny overboard for a strong wind, and finally throwing a penny overboard and saying, "black pig" at the same time for a real blast.

Our skipper would have none of it. He knew that the knife, the penny, and the incantation were all as likely as not to produce a wind strong enough to blow out the sails, and with the price of sailcloth being what it was, he wasn't taking any chances with that. He had a better method—recite random verses from Samuel Taylor Coleridge's *Rime of the Ancient Mariner* ("I never set sail without a copy"), the theory being that you read a verse out loud and see what happens. If nothing, read another. If that produces only a zephyr, read another. Simply keep on reading, with pauses to check the effect, until the desired level of wind has been achieved.

"Silence, please," the skipper said, opening a ragged edition of Coleridge to the first of several marked pages. He took off his cap and put on a pair of reading glasses.

> *Down dropt the breeze, the sails dropt down,*
> *'Twas sad as sad could be;*
> *And we did speak only to break*
> *The silence of the sea!*

We live in the modern age. We believe in science, we believe in meteorology, we believe in the absolutes of digital readouts from black boxes stuffed with semiconductors. We believe the analysts in the employ of the Coast Guard and the National Transportation Safety Board when they tell us that untoward circumstances aboard ships at sea are caused by none other than failure to pay attention to proper safety procedures. We believe a huge tanker went aground off Valdez, Alaska, causing the biggest oil spill in American history, because of pilot error or too much liquor at the wrong time or failure to set the radar screen at the proper scale or something like that. We would call for the white truck and the attendants with straitjackets if the commandant of the Coast Guard stood up at a press conference and announced that the reason why the *Exxon Valdez* went on the rocks was that the skipper was wearing red mittens or the trim of the vessel's superstructure was painted blue. Yet not that long ago—and still among some sailors today—there was the belief that tragedy was caused by bad luck, and that bad luck was produced by certain carelessnesses.

Day after day, day after day,
We stuck, nor breath nor motion;
As idle as a painted ship
Upon a painted ocean.

There was a long string of "nevers," things a sailor must never do or allow to be done. Never depart on a Friday or launch a vessel on a Friday or allow the keel of a new vessel to be laid on a Friday. Never wear red mittens or stockings or mufflers, especially in a shipyard where a new vessel was under construction, and never paint any trim on a vessel blue. Never turn a hatch cover bottom-up. Never watch a departing ship out of sight. Never sail aboard a ship that stuck on the ways when it was launched or had a bootjack on board. Never whistle while underway or drive a nail on a Sunday, as a gale will be the certain result.

The very deep did rot: O Christ!
That ever this should be!
Yea, slimy things did crawl with legs
Upon the slimy sea.

There were, however, ways to banish bad luck. It was said, for example, that on the first voyage of the season, a vessel should set sail to the northward for good luck. Even if the vessel's course were to the south or the east or the west, even if there were a foul wind or tide from the north, she should first sail northward, however briefly. If that principle were violated, there was no telling the horrors of the consequences.

Alone, alone, all, all alone,
Alone on a wide wide sea!
And never a saint took pity on
My soul in agony.

It was said, for another example, that good luck could be brought upon a vessel if a horseshoe were nailed, open end up, to the end of the bowsprit. If a horseshoe so affixed were to fall off during the course of a voyage, tragedy would befall the vessel and her crew.

But soon there breathed a wind on me,
Nor sound nor motion made:
Its path was not upon the sea,
In ripple or in shade.

It was said on the coast of Maine that there were people imbued with the ingredients to ensure good luck and that those people should be treated with the proper respect. "A

Protected from possible foul weather from any direction, the *J. & E. Riggin* has found a snug anchorage for the night.

certain woman, renowned for her ability to control weather and to furnish general good fortune to seafarers, lived alone a mile or more back from the shore," wrote George Wasson. "It was well worth while to keep Aunt Polly supplied with tea, tobacco and snuff, to buy of her heavy knit stockings, mittens or 'nippers,' and to see that her woodpile never unduly diminished. Trips up to Aunt Polly's small dwelling, with offerings given and purchases made, often preceded trips to the Grand Banks or to Bangor. Quoth a man…'Maybe there wan't nothin' so very much in it, but to the last day of my goin' coastin' to 'Bangor River,' I always kind of felt better-like when things had been fixed up good and plenty with old Aunt Polly.'"

Swiftly, swiftly flew the ship,
Yet she sailed softly too:
Sweetly, sweetly blew the breeze—
On me alone it blew.

✸

The schooner's snug hole was to be Southeast Harbor on Deer Isle, at the eastern end of the Deer Island Thorofare. The approaches from Jericho Bay were full of ledges and small islands, but the chart showed a large harbor well inside bounded by Stinson and Whitmore necks, which would provide protection from virtually all directions.

By suppertime, when we still had a few more miles to go to our anchorage, our once-gentle breeze had turned to a raw, cold, and penetrating wind that blew hard from the east. The cook rang the dinner bell and the passengers trooped happily below to the warmth of the galley stove, leaving the skipper and the mate and me alone under the darkening

The main cabin of the *Adventure*.

sky to sail the rest of the way. The clouds were low and raggedy, and the tumbling seas had angry whitecaps with spray driven off their tops. Rain lashed the deck and ran down our necks. The cook's helper brought up an oilcloth-covered tray and left it on top of the main cabinhouse. Hot biscuits and steaming coffee—a full-fledged meal would have to wait until later.

Before us was a sight not easily forgotten: the wet, empty decks; the glow of the running lights in the rigging; the rain running off the sails; the white, boiling wake; the skipper in his black Lunenburg fisherman-style oilskins and seaboots; the mate up forward pulling the canvas cover off the windlass and flaking down the glistening anchor chain; the surf breaking on the ledges; the buoys pushed over on their sides by the tidal current and the weight of the rising storm; the dim lights of the houses in the little villages of Sunshine and Oceanville.

We sailed deep into Southeast Harbor, as far as we could go and still have sufficient water at low tide to float the vessel. There were no other schooners inside—"I bet Bucks, Pulpit, and Burnt Coat are crowded tonight," the skipper said—and only a few lobsterboats. Not a yacht in sight. We came up into the wind and let go the anchor; then the mate called down the companionway hatch for volunteers to help furl the sails. There was no stampede, you can be sure of that.

After supper, there was singing in the main cabin and cribbage in the galley under the soft amber glow of the kerosene lanterns. And then the skipper set a pot of fresh-brewed coffee on the table and told stories, some apocryphal and some not, about the coast of Maine in the days of wooden ships and iron men. As he spoke, the wind moaned in the rigging and the rain pounded on the deck above and the schooner swayed to the force of the gale. Outside, in the thickening storm, it was a black, black night.

The galley of the *Heritage*.

VII *A Town by the Edge of the Sea*

At many spots along the coast and rivers nature has provided granite with so lavish a hand that it lies almost on the surface ready to be taken. It was not even necessary to quarry deeply for it. When Dix, Hurricane, Fox and Crotch Islands, and Stonington in Penobscot Bay ... are mentioned, the Maine Coast man thinks of granite.
—William Hutchinson Rowe, *The Maritime History of Maine*

It was a restless, thrashing, wringing-wet night, the wind blowing out of the east and the northeast and the north in gusts as high as 50-some-odd knots, the temperature down in the fifties, the atmosphere penetratingly raw. Sheets of rain, almost horizontal at times, smashed against the schooner, and moisture worked its way below through deck seams, mast boots, ventilators, portlights, companionway hatches, any and all unsealed openings. But the crew kept the woodstove fires stoked in the galley and the main cabin, and in those compartments, at least, a cheerful, reasonably dry warmth prevailed.

Not so on deck. Rain and spray, thunder and lightning, wind shrieking in the rigging, halyards slapping so sharply and rapidly against the masts that the sound was like machine guns during the fiercest battles on the Western Front. The vessel rolled and lurched to the storm. The skipper and mate were up nearly the entire night, securing loose gear, checking the rigging (especially the anchor chain) for chafe, and watching for the slightest sign that the anchors (two had been set) might be dragging. Despite full suits of foulweather gear, including thick towels around their necks to fight off the rain, they were soaked to the skin and remained that way no matter how often they ducked below to stand by the galley stove and drink strong tea and have a quick smoke.

The storm blew itself out a couple of hours before dawn. Like the crescendo at a fireworks display, the end came with a series of thunder-and-lightning salutes and several discrete blasts of wind that were strong enough to peel your eyelids back. Then, as if someone had ripped a curtain aside, the stars appeared in the blackest of black skies. The skipper and the mate, exhausted, stumbled below. They pulled off their sodden clothes, hung them to dry in the galley, and fell into their bunks for a few hours' rest.

Thursday morning, the entire schooner awoke at once. The alarm was the happy sound of the northwest wind breezing through the rigging. The cook threw back the companionway hatches, and a river of cold, dry air flowed through the hull and drove out the

Early risers greet the sun after a stormy night at anchor.

dampness in a matter of minutes. The sun was out—not a cloud in the sky—and the air had that delicious braciness to it, like dry cider, that is common to Canada in late September, Vermont in mid-October, western Virginia in early November. Fall had struck like a woodsman's ax, even though the equinox was technically three weeks away. Foulweather gear was happily abandoned, and flannel shirts and woolen sweaters and warm socks were pulled with relish from the bottoms of seabags.

Cold autumn air or not, several swimmers were out before breakfast, doing laps around the schooner as the rest of the passengers cheered them on. A woman emerged from the galley with a pail of hot water and offered her services as a rinser for those who wished to wash their hair under the saltwater hose by the forward cabinhouse. Most of the men who hadn't shaved yet during the week got out soap and razors and scraped and hacked in front of a mirror that had been tacked to the foremast. It was that kind of a morning. A new beginning.

At breakfast the skipper, spruced up somewhat by a clean red-checked shirt, snapped his suspenders and announced that the first order of business was to clear out of Southeast Harbor, sail down the Deer Island Thorofare, and pay a visit to the friendly neighborhood fish and crustacean dealer. "Lobster and steamed clams on the beach tonight," he said. "Sweet corn, too, if Bartlett's Market has any in. Maine crazy pudding for dessert if you're nice to the cook!"

"Cold autumn air or not, several swimmers were out before breakfast, doing laps around the schooner."

Our schooner came upon the town suddenly. We were on the Deer Island Thorofare, just past Buckmaster Neck and Webb Cove. The Thorofare, a long channel separating the major island of Deer Isle from the lesser islands of Merchant Row, had the feel of a highway—a liquid one, not an asphalt one.

One minute we were surrounded by the wild, lonely emptiness of the coast, the surf left by the storm foaming around the ledges and the sea under the unobscured sun the color of a bluebottle fly. The next minute, after passing a point, we were brought up short by the appearance, as in a knee-buckling vision, of the archetypal Maine-coast town perched on the edge of the sea. The houses, almost all of them shingled or white, were crowded together without logical pattern on the slope of a steep, ledgy hill. The largest building, as old-fashioned looking as a Model A Ford, carried a painted sign—Opera House.—punctuated in the nineteenth-century manner. It was a down-home, downtown, down-east, finestkind, first-rate, working-class, island fishing town. So authentic, so unbelievably salty that—to borrow a phrase from a colleague—just looking at it could make your eyes rust.

"What is this town?" one of the passengers asked.

"Stonington," the skipper said, "You'll have to look long and hard to find a more authentic town on the coast of Maine, and if you do, it'll probably be in Canada."

By the looks of things, Fishington would have been a better name. The harbor, open to the south with a clear, unobstructed view of the islands of Merchant Row and Isle au Haut on the horizon, was packed with fishing boats and other commercial craft. There were no yachts. The shore was ringed with piers, docks, wharves, bait shacks, chandleries, fish buyers, boatyards, and a packing plant. A full-bore fishing town with a couple of schooners for good measure. The dark-green-hulled schooner *Stephen Taber* was lying to an anchor with her reefed main still set; she was cocked into the wind like a weathervane atop a horse barn on a saltwater farm. The schooner *American Eagle*, with a sheer that wouldn't quit, was anchored nearby.

One of the last fishing schooners to be built on the east coast, the *American Eagle* was launched back in 1930 in Gloucester, Massachusetts, as the *Andrew and Rosalie*. She was soon converted to an eastern-rigged dragger—which is to say, her rig was cut down, a big engine was installed, and a pilothouse was erected on her afterdeck. (Western-rigged draggers have their pilothouses up forward. Both types fish by dragging open-mouthed nets across the ocean floor. In recent years, the eastern dragger has fallen out of favor, the western rig being much preferred for the better visibility it offers the helmsman and for the clear afterdeck for handling the fishing gear.) Retired from fishing in 1983, the *American Eagle* was bought by Captain John Foss, formerly of the *Lewis R. French*, rebuilt to her schooner configuration, and fitted with an auxiliary engine. Her first season in the windjammer fleet was 1986.

We sailed into the harbor with all sails set and cast our anchor between the two schooners that had preceded us. "Schooner sandwich," the skipper yelled over to Captain Barnes on the *Taber*. "You and Foss are the bread. We," he said with a mock bow, "are the meat."

A crowd of schooners
waiting for a chance-along.
In the foreground is the
Mary Day, decked out with
a new set of colors.

"Yeah," said Captain Barnes, returning the bow, "turkey meat."

Luckily for us, our skipper didn't hear the remark, or if he did, he wasn't letting on. Despite the magnificent weather, he had been in a foul mood all morning because of his lack of sleep the night before. ("Look at those 'contemporary' houses," he had said, pointing out a pair of A-frames cantilevered over an otherwise-unspoiled ledge. "You know what they should do with them? Burn them. Or send them back to Sugarloaf.")

In half an hour, with the exception of the mate and galley hand, who remained behind to stand watch, the ship's company was ashore. The skipper and the cook went over to the fishermen's co-op to arrange for lobsters and clams; a gang of passengers went off to a little waterfront motel to rent a room collectively and take hot showers; and everyone else took full advantage of the first chance to range unfettered around a genuine full-service town.

Stonington was as good as any coastal town to be set loose in, though "full-service" may be slightly overstating the situation. We found a drugstore and a market (Bartlett's) and a classic dry-goods store (Epstein's), a couple of tiny motels, several tourist shops, a summer-only restaurant, and two year-round eating establishments that drew customers from miles around—Connie's and the Fisherman's Friend, up on the hill. Just about everything else—the supply stores, the cannery, the buyers, the boatyards, the engine repair shops—related to the fishing industry.

Stonington is a town with a rep, if you know what I mean—a place of legend, part apocryphal, part not. Townspeople of independent mind—clannish, standoffish, unfriendly to outsiders. Rum-running during Prohibition and the occasional drug-running now. Lobstermen arguing among themselves over hereditary rights to certain territories for setting their traps and settling their differences with fists and crowbars and knives and shotguns. Fishermen in Rockland and Vinalhaven, no slouches themselves when push comes to shove, speak of their Stonington brethren with a certain wary respect: "They're a rough, tough bunch over there, that's for sure."

Which means, of course, that of all the cruise schooners' ports of call, Stonington comes the closest to providing the feel of the coasting harbors of the Golden Era—a fact that the townspeople, who are proud of their heritage, love and hate at the same time. To outsiders, visitors "from away"—"outlanders" as the locals sometimes call them—the town, as small as it is, has a certain intensity, an excitement of being the center of the surrounding territory, of commerce, of the place where everything that matters is going to happen. There's the feeling of being on a frontier, an edge, a far, far distance from the larger, "real," world. It's one of those towns where you can hear your own footsteps in the middle of the day and where everything goes silent as a north-country forest in the late afternoon, when the fishermen's co-op shuts down and the lobster buyers go home and the post office closes for the day.

It is a new town as New England towns go, the majority of the buildings having been built just before and after the turn of the century, when Stonington, like other coastal island communities, was at the height of its powers. Originally called Green's Landing, it was a tiny settlement of saltwater farmers and fishermen on the rim of a minor cove at the tip of Deer Isle. But in the late nineteenth century, a substantial granite-quarrying industry employing hundreds of people took hold in the area, especially on several of the smaller, nearby islands, and Green's Landing became a seaport and the seaport came to be named for the stone shipped to the westward. But modern construction techniques came to rely less on cut stone and more on precast concrete, so most of the quarries closed a few decades ago, most of the stonecutters left, all of the coasting schooners disappeared, and most of the townspeople who remained joined the fishermen or the industries that supported them. (The only quarry still in business is across the Thorofare on Crotch Island; where once its workforce numbered in the hundreds, now it employs about half a dozen full-time workers.)

Evidence of the old quarries is everywhere around Stonington, which was constructed on, by, and for stone. The houses are built on stone ledges; the foundations are of cut stone. There are stone walls, wharves, curbs, moorings, and, of course, headstones in the cemeteries—though surprisingly, the markers, even for some of the great quarrymen, are far less elegant than one would expect. Perhaps the townspeople were too busy cutting stone for the monuments and bridges and buildings of New York City and couldn't find the time to make monuments to themselves.

❂

Stonington is a deceptive town to the visitor. It seems backward in the most pleasant sense of the word, a throwback to the turn of the century, a Mystic Seaport or—dare I say it?—a Disney World of the coast. To outsiders it looks as if it were put there primarily to make the tourists feel good and only secondarily to provide a home and hearth for the inhabitants. Similar towns on the coast of Maine—Boothbay Harbor, Camden, Bar Harbor—understand that notion and cater to it. After all, there's money to be made by stocking bait shacks with native art manufactured in Hong Kong and chandleries with T-shirts and soft-serve ice cream. But in Stonington the local people see their town differently, and, like a diminishing number of fishing communities along the coast, they are quick to protect their interests.

Not to say that they have been entirely successful. There are several small stores, open only during the summer, for the tourists, and many choice pieces of waterfront property have changed hands recently. Most of the fishermen are convinced that ten years from now the commercial wharves and piers will be in the hands of the outsiders and the only place left for them will be the new municipal fish pier. But for the most part, the prevailing attitude of the townspeople is that authenticity is the most important aspect of the community to be preserved. As far as they are concerned, working lobsterboats are unpretentious and utilitarian and therefore authentic, and the people who own and work on them share the same characteristics. Yachts and other pleasure craft are all gussied up and not what they appear to be and therefore unauthentic, and their owners and guests are ditto.

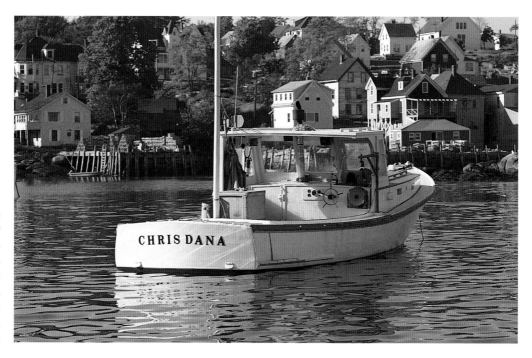

Stonington, at the southern end of Deer Isle, is a full-bore fishing town. The harbor is circled with wharves, bait shacks, chandleries, fish buyers, boatyards, and a packing plant.

Oftentimes, the people of Stonington will go out of their way to make this attitude obvious. "It's a game, a show," a resident said. "On nights in the summer when the schooners are in town, part of the sport for some of the people is to go down to the harbor and entertain themselves by poking fun at the outlandish outlanders."

Like genuine islanders all along the coast of Maine, they are open and unpolished—an almost universal characteristic—and make little attempt to cover up their feelings. If you ignore the sidewalk and walk down the middle of the street (a temptation few tourists in Stonington can resist), if you talk out loud about the "cute little town" and the "quaint, old-fashioned fishermen," if you insinuate in any way that island life is somehow culturally substandard, then you will hear about it. You might not be tarred and feathered and run out of town on a rail, but your life could be made so miserable that you might as well have been.

The townspeople of Stonington have never been happy with the common perception by outsiders that they are quaint, not particularly smart rustics living in a charming little nineteenth-century village not much bigger than half a city block, with bait barrels on one side and overgrown Christmas trees on the other. In fact, if the truth be known, they hate that perception. In their minds, they are normal people, living normal working people's lives. (Well, not totally, if a bumper sticker on a truck at Conary's Wharf is any indication: Work Is for People Who Don't Know How to Fish.) Like anyone else anywhere else, they get up in the morning, go to work, put in an honest day's labor, come home, eat supper, entertain themselves for the evening, go to bed, get up the next morning and do it all over again. They do not see themselves as unique. Threatened, perhaps, but not unique.

The threat comes from two directions. The first is the Deer Isle Bridge, which connects the northern end of the island with the mainland. The second is our schooner and others like it, which dump scores of passengers right in the middle of town. And by historical accident, both threats originally came to pass coincidentally. The bridge was opened in the summer of 1938 and the use of coasting schooners ("skinboats" in the Stonington vernacular) to carry vacationing passengers developed at just about the same time. They came by land and they came by sea.

Bridge or no bridge, the people of Stonington and Deer Isle still see themselves as islanders, not mainlanders. They are out of the mainstream and like it, or they would have moved a long time ago to Ellsworth or Bangor or Rockland or somewhere else where goods and services and the conveniences of modern-day life are more readily available. But don't get me wrong. The townspeople don't hate the bridge; in fact, back in 1938 they paused for perhaps a microsecond to regret the passing of the familiar ferry service across Eggemoggin Reach and then did a half-gainer smack into the pool of mainland accessibility. What they do regret—at least the vast majority of islanders who make their living in a sphere other than tourism—is that people on the mainland, especially tourists who like to visit quaint fishing villages, have every right to use the bridge, too, and exercise that right in increasing numbers.

It isn't the tourists themselves who strike fear into the hearts of Stonington residents. It is a fear of the changes the tourists are likely to make on the character of the town, as well as a corollary apprehension that too many tourists might take a liking to the place, buy some property, and stick around. For example, when a small, unassuming restaurant down by the fish factory was sold a few years ago to an outsider, who upgraded the establishment so it now caters to tourists and summer people, the year-rounders voted against the change by withholding their patronage. After all, the people of Stonington know who they are and what their town is: working class, pure and simple. Historically, prosperity or the lack of it has always depended on blue-collar employment—stonecutting, boatbuilding, fishing, carpentry, mechanics—and has had little dependence on white-collar jobs, tourism, and entertainment.

But change is creeping up on Stonington, just as it is penetrating into the other farthest

A lobsterboat underway off Stonington.

reaches of Maine. There are, for example, as many real estate brokers as fish buyers in town, whereas not that long ago, the ratio was heavily weighted in favor of the buyers. Yet there's something about the Stonington attitude that indicates the community will survive once again, just as it survived the transition from a stonecutter's and schoonerman's town to that of the fisherman when the big quarries went out of business. There is indeed an unpleasant element in the town, a rawboned fierceness that surfaces from time to time when pressures—primarily political and social—build up and demand release, but without that, Stonington would be just another coastal town: unbearably crowded in the summer and boarded up and empty in the winter—a pretty little village with a view.

✴

The view! I climbed to the brow of the hill behind the town. If there were a more stupendous scene on the coast of Maine, I have never seen it. The wharves, the gulls circling the fishing fleet, the green-blue sea, the granite shore, the spruce-capped islands, the great bulk of Isle au Haut.

The *Stephen Taber* had set all sail and hauled up her anchor and was heading out of the harbor wing-and-wing downwind. The crew of the *American Eagle* was sweating up her sails, preparing to get underway. I could hear the shouts of the mate ("Let's go, one more time....Heave!"), the auxiliary engine ticking over, the sheaves turning in the wooden-shelled blocks, the gaff jaws and mast hoops sliding up the masts. I imagined I could smell the tar in the rigging and the cotton canvas of the sun-bleached sails and the linseed oil on the decks and the coffee percolating down in the galley. An hour or two away from our schooner and I was already homesick.

The *American Eagle*'s flags and pennants snapped in the breeze. From where I stood, on a side street under a maple tree next to a white-clapboard Maine-style two-story house with yellow mums growing by the walkway, in one of the few remaining New England towns with heart, looking down on a maritime scene right out of a Winslow Homer painting, it could have been fifty or seventy-five years ago. If the power lobsterboats had been sailing sloopboats and smacks and the streets of the town had been dirt, it could have been a hundred years ago or more.

I walked over to the Fisherman's Friend for a cup of coffee and a fried-haddock sandwich, and then followed a winding road through the back of town to Billings Diesel & Marine, the largest single business in Stonington, employing about half a hundred people. On a small island tucked behind Green Head, the boatyard is connected to the town by a causeway with a lobster pound on each side. Billings is primarily a commercial fisherman's yard, building and repairing in steel, wood, fiberglass, whatever the fishermen want. In addition, it serves many of Maine's cruise schooners and larger vessels from all parts of the New England coast. Yachts, too, but you won't find very many people in Stonington bragging about that.

There was a time, not that long ago, when scores of yards along the coast of Maine could handle large vessels. Any harbor worthy of a name had at least one marine railway, and

The *American Eagle*, one of the last fishing schooners built on the east coast. She was soon converted to a power dragger, but in the mid-1980s, following her retirement, she was rerigged as a sailing vessel.

A lobster pound in the foreground, Billings Diesel & Marine in the background. Billings, just on the other side of Green Head from Stonington, is one of the few boatyards with adequate facilities for hauling large schooners.

usually several, for hauling coasting schooners and sailing fishermen, but along with the decline of the fleet came a decline of the institutions that served the fleet: the building and repair yards, the sawmills, the sail and rigging lofts, the chandleries, the shipsmiths, the sawmills. Today, the yards that have the facilities for hauling and servicing a schooner such as ours are few and far between: Billings in Stonington, Wayfarer Marine in Camden, Snow's and the North End Shipyard in Rockland, and Sample's in Boothbay Harbor. There are a few others, but they are too expensive or don't understand the particular care a wooden vessel requires, or both. It's one thing to work on fiberglass, aluminum, and steel fishing vessels; it's quite another to work on wood.

Unlike yachts and lobsterboats and other small craft, the big schooners are not hauled for dry storage during the off-season months. Rather, they are left in the water year round. Wet storage is better for several reasons, not the least of which is that it is cheaper than laying up the vessel in a yard. The most important reason, however, is that a schooner in the water doesn't dry out, a condition that hastens the end of a large wooden hull; the planking shrinks, the wood checks, the seams open up, and the joints become loose. It is true that a dried-out hull will swell again when put back into the water, but after several cycles of wet and dry, the hull will lose its resilience. Better to leave the vessel in the water and maintain it there—with the exception of a brief haulout, usually in the spring, to work on the bottom.

At the end of the season—usually in mid- to late October—the sails are unbent, topmasts sent down, and running rigging removed. As much as possible is stored in a warehouse ashore, and what isn't is carefully secured and protected against the winter weather. To keep rain, snow, and ice off the vessels, temporary wood-framed shelters covered with sheet plastic are erected over the hulls. Stripped down, covered over, fendered and buffered for protection against ice and other hazards, the schooners are moored with heavy lines in protected corners of such harbors as Camden, Rockport, and Rockland. Most are fitted with automatic bilge pumps or alarms to warn the owner if the bilge water rises too high. On occasion, a shipkeeper might live aboard, but it takes an iron constitution to set up housekeeping in a damp, drafty schooner in a lonely winter harbor with the wind howling out of the north and the temperature below zero.

A laid-up schooner may look alone and abandoned, but such is not the case. Most owners work on the vessels during the winter months, the plastic cover serving as a shop roof, the translucent material yielding sufficient light and a certain amount of solar warmth during the day. A woodstove, its exhaust pipe exiting through the plastic cover, provides additional heat. At Christmastime, an evergreen is hoisted to the masthead to prove that, indeed, life goes on.

At winter's end—which in Maine can come anytime between mid-March and late April—the cover is stripped off and spring fitting-out can begin. Scraping, sanding, painting, varnishing, oiling, going over the above-water planking, setting up the rigging, and bending on the sails, the crew works for weeks to get the vessel shipshape for the coming season. Sooner or later, the schooner is towed over to a marine railway to be hauled so the bottom can be maintained (the Coast Guard requires hull inspection at least once every eighteen months): planking and fastenings inspected, caulking renewed as necessary, and antifouling paint applied. For years, Billings was the yard of choice, but since the founding of Rockland's North End Shipyard in 1973, many of the schooners are hauled out there because it is so much closer to their homeports.

But every year one or two schooners opt for old-style careening—running the vessel onto a soft, protected shore at high water and waiting for the tide to go out. The vessel is allowed to lay over, resting on the turn of the bilge, and the exposed side of the bottom is scraped and painted. On the next high tide, the vessel is turned, and at the low tide that follows, six hours later, the other side of the bottom is scraped and painted. Only a sound wooden vessel can be careened, as the strain on the hull—unsupported except on the side edge of the keel and the turn of the bilge—is considerable. In the old days, some of the smaller schooners were laid alongside wharves and tied securely to bollards. When the tide went out, they would be standing upright, which was fine for vessels that were rather V-shaped in section, as the bottom would be reasonably accessible to the crew, but it was not much good for U-shaped vessels, since the bottom of the U would be resting in the mud.

I have watched the *Mary Day* and the *Stephen Taber* careened at the head of the harbor in Camden, and "picturesque" is hardly the word to describe the operation. The schooner heeled way over so her masts jut over the green grass of the town park, the crew in knee-high rubber boots mucking around in the low-tide mud, the frantic scraping with big iron tools, painting with rollers on long wooden poles and brushes as big as floor mops, the apprehension of the skipper—"The tide, the tide! Are we going to make this tide?"—the photographers and videotapers recording a scene as old as seafaring itself.

An hour after noon, the skipper and the cook were at the town landing, the yawlboat packed with lobsters (almost 100 pounds, enough for two critters per person), clams, sweet corn, and three huge watermelons. The price of the lobsters had been high for this time of year, three dollars a pound—at least twenty-five cents more than it would have been at the dealer's in Burnt Coat Harbor. The skipper said he wished he had put in there.

"You're looking at almost four hundred dollars in groceries for one meal," he said. "No wonder me and the wife eat a lot of B&M baked beans in the winter."

The news from the waterfront had to do with a couple of fishing boats that had been driven ashore during the storm—one had been pulled off successfully, with moderate, fixable damage; the other had been pulverized between two giant boulders—and a set-to earlier in the week between a local lobsterman and the skipper of one of the cruise schooners. It seemed that a large vessel—perhaps a schooner, perhaps not—had sailed through a patch of lobster-trap buoys down by Isle au Haut and destroyed a considerable amount of valuable gear. The lobsterman, who was out several hundred dollars, blamed the "goddam skinboats" and took out his anger on the next one to anchor in the narrow Thorofare between Kimball Island and Isle au Haut. He hauled off and intentionally rammed the side of the schooner with his lobsterboat; the schooner's skipper, who knew nothing of the lost gear, almost got into a fistfight. A lot of angry words and threats passed back and forth before the lobsterman backed off.

"Figures," the skipper said, getting hot under the collar as he related the story. "When something goes wrong, blame the biggest convenient thing to hand. None of us like to have potwarps wrapped around our rudders and centerboards. What the hell does he think we do? See a bunch of pot buoys and head right for them? Plus I'd like to point out to that fellow that the so-called goddam skinboats buy a lot of lobsters around here and that ought to count for something."

As he spoke, the schooner *Mistress* emerged from behind Green Head and put in to Stonington for lobsters and clams. One of the "green boats," she was, at 40 feet on deck, the smallest vessel in the schooner fleet. Her construction was begun in 1960 by an amateur builder on Deer Isle, but in the tradition of so many part-time backyard boatbuilders, he never finished. Captain Jim Nisbet bought the hull in 1966, took it over to Camden, and finished it off as a miniature cruise schooner—tiny, slower than cold molasses, odd-looking in many respects, but a cute little craft nevertheless for her ship-model-like qualities. She carried a crew of two, with three staterooms for two passengers each, the perfect vessel for six friends sailing together.

We watched the *Mistress* come to anchor smartly off the fishermen's co-op wharf, embarked the last of our passengers, motored out to our schooner, stowed the supper supplies down in the galley, and got underway. It was a perfect afternoon for sailing. A hard, dry breeze from the northwest. Smooth water in the lee of the islands. Sunlight reflected like dancing diamonds on the surface of the sea. The sharp smell of seaweed in the air. Perfect.

"The perfect vessel for six friends
sailing together." The *Mistress*.

VIII *"Oh, How She Scoons!"*

*Among other things [the schooner captain] told me was never
to look at the dancing sunlight on the water, and especially
the dancing moonlight. It will turn you inside out in a minute.*
                                    —Frederick Sturgis Laurence

We sailed west on the Thorofare, between Crotch Island and Green Head out into East
Penobscot Bay toward Vinalhaven, which was shimmering like a jeweled gown in the
bright sun. Up the bay we could see Butter and Eagle islands; down the bay the lighthouse
on Saddleback Ledge; and way off in the distance to the south, the low smudge of Seal
Island on the horizon.

"Take off your hats and bow your heads," the skipper said when we entered the square
patch of sea cornered by Mark Island, West Mark Island Ledge, Scraggy Island, and The
Brown Cow. "Somewhere below us lie the mortal remains of the *Lydia M. Webster*, one
of the first schooners in the Maine windjammer fleet." The *Webster* was, in fact, Captain
Swift's second vessel, and, like most of the early passenger-carrying schooners, she was
discarded after her better days were over. In 1945, her crew punched holes in the hull
below the waterline and allowed her to sink to the bottom of the bay.

The *Lydia M. Webster* died in an era when there were so many sailing cargo vessels
to be had for next to nothing that it did not pay to rebuild tired-out cruise schooners. It
didn't even pay to maintain them properly. The easiest and most economical approach
was to wear them out, then strip off all the useful gear—sails, blocks, deadeyes, compasses,
spars, ironwork, anchors, stoves, steering wheels, davits—and get rid of them. There were
plenty more where those came from. They were seen as wretched, broken-down, unim-
portant, valueless, used-up, useless bags of bones.

The *Webster* was lucky. Her burial at sea was at least reasonably dignified, though it
is not known whether or not her owner held a memorial service after the plug was pulled.
Most cruise schooners met their end as if they were no more important than old junk left
over after the annual Lion's Club yard sale. The lovely *Alice S. Wentworth*, 1863—"I
suppose every man (or boy) who ever went to sea had a favorite vessel," wrote John F.
Leavitt. "Mine was the then handsome *Alice S. Wentworth*."—was tied to a restaurant
wharf in Boston as an example of Ye Olde Shippe from Ye Olde Tymes of Yore until she

"A schooner is
nothing more than
a vessel with two or
more masts, the after
mast as tall as or
taller than the fore,
and with principal
sails of the fore-and-
aft type—triangular
or quadrilateral in
shape—in other
words, they are
not squaresails."
The *Roseway*.

sank and had to be broken up and removed. Ditto for the *Lois M. Candage*, 1912, which rotted alongside a restaurant in Damariscotta, Maine.

The *Lillian*, 1876, was beached and broken up at Sandy Point. The *Annie F. Kimball*, 1886, was abandoned on the shore of Camden's inner harbor and eventually went to pieces of her own accord. The end for the *Enterprise*, 1909, came more quickly; she was hauled ashore in Camden and burned. The *Mabel*, 1881, Captain Swift's first windjammer, in terminal disrepair, sank of her own accord off Maine's Seguin Island. The *Clinton*, 1886, rotted to nothing in a Stonington boatyard. So, too, the *Eva S. Cullison*, 1888, on the shore of Cape Ann, Massachusetts. The *Maggie*, 1871, was left by a wharf in Rockland, Maine, and ultimately burned. The *Grace & Alice*, 1910, was laid up at Carney Island and stripped by vandals. By the standards of today, a time of increasing awareness of the value of maritime preservation, it was a shameless waste of historic vessels—no matter the perception of their condition.

Perception, of course, is everything. In the 1930s, '40s, '50s—even for most of the 1960s—old wooden ships were perceived as nothing more than old wooden ships, valueless hulks that had been superseded by superior vessels and therefore seldom given a thought. The sooner they were gone, the sooner the seas and waterfronts would be free of a bunch of unreconstructable eyesores. Never mind that these vessels were living links with our past; never mind that they represented a maritime tradition that had once been so strong that trivialization by destruction bordered on the criminal. They were like the old buildings in Boston and Bangor, T Wharf and the Portland Railroad Station, burned and torn apart and allowed to collapse in on themselves and then replaced by something "better."

✦

The schooner tradition may only amount to a low rise on the larger sweep of the landscape of American history, but it nevertheless goes back to the earliest days of our country. The schooner rig itself is several centuries old, and its use to propel vessels in coastwise commerce can be traced back at least to the seventeenth century in the Old World and the early eighteenth century in the New. (It is thought that the first schooners were pleasure craft, but experts are not in total agreement on that.)

The term *schooner* refers to a vessel with a certain type of rig, although over the years, vessels so rigged have developed a hull form that has "schooner" written all over them. Anyone familiar with the type can identify a Grand Banks fishing schooner, for example, on sight, even if the rig has been cut down and deck structures have been added. So, too, the coasting and pilot schooners. But, technically speaking, a schooner is nothing more than a vessel with two or more masts, the after mast as tall as or taller than the fore, and with principal sails of the fore-and-aft type—triangular or quadrilateral in shape—in other words, not squaresails. In the nineteenth century, there were many schooners (known generically as topsail schooners) that carried square topsails and sometimes even topgallant sails on the foremast in addition to the fore-and-aft type, but such squaresails

The pinky
schooner
Summertime.

were only secondary. (Most British schooners were rigged with squaresails on the foremast, as were the legendary Baltimore clippers.) Today a few schooners, primarily foreign, carry square topsails on the foremast, though none in the Maine windjammer fleet carry such a rig.

Nobody has successfully pinpointed the origin of the schooner rig, though plenty of historians have tried. The earliest-known illustration of a schooner is by a Dutch artist named Rool, whose pen-and-ink drawing shows the yacht of the burgomasters of Amsterdam. The vessel is shown running before the wind, wing-and-wing; she carries fore-and-aft sails with short gaffs at the head; the foremast, shorter than the mainmast, is set way forward. There is no bowsprit; no staysail or jib. The date is 1600.

There are a few eighteenth-century illustrations extant of schooners in American waters, the most famous being a Paul Revere engraving showing Boston Harbor at the beginning of the American Revolution. Among the vessels in the anchorage are several schooners, including two without square topsails. One is at anchor and the other is underway; both look much like schooners seen today along the Maine coast.

Most historians agree that the schooner rig originated in Europe—probably somewhere in the Netherlands in the sixteenth or seventeenth centuries—and was brought over to America in the normal course of colonization. Yet there is a belief that the rig was invented in Gloucester, Massachusetts, in 1713, by Captain Andrew Robinson—evidence of an earlier European origin notwithstanding. This theory was published in 1860 in the *History of the Town of Gloucester, Cape Ann*, by John J. Babson:

A current tradition of the town relates the origin of the "schooner"; and abundant testimony, of both a positive and negative kind, confirms the story so strongly, that it is unnecessary to take further notice of the verbal account. Dr. Moses Prince, brother of the annalist, writing in this town, Sept. 25, 1721, says, "Went to see Captain Robinson's lady, &c. This gentleman was the first contriver of schooners, and built the first of the sort about eight years since; and the use that is now made of them, being so much known, has convinced the world of their convenience beyond other vessels, and shows how mankind is obliged to this gentleman for this knowledge." Nearly seventy years afterwards, another visitor gives some further particulars of this interesting fact. Cotton Tufts, Esq., connected with us by marriage, being in Gloucester, September 8, 1790, writes: "I was informed (and committed the same to writing) that the kind of vessels called 'schooners' derived their name from this circumstance: viz., Mr. Andrew Robinson of that place, having constructed a vessel which he masted and rigged in the same manner as schooners are at this day, on her going off the stocks and passing into the water, a bystander cried out, 'Oh, how she scoons!' Robinson instantly replied, 'A scooner let her be!' From which time, vessels thus masted and rigged have gone by the name of 'schooners'; before which, vessels of this description were not known in Europe nor America. This account was confirmed to me by a great number of persons in Gloucester." The strongest negative evidence corroborates these statements. No marine dictionary, no commercial record, no merchant's inventory, of a date prior to 1713, containing the word "schooner" has yet been discovered; and it may, therefore, be received as an historical fact, that the first vessel of this class had her origin in Gloucester, as stated by the respectable authorities above cited.

Howard Chapelle, the leading historian of naval architecture in America, called the theory of the Gloucester invention of the schooner "a childish fable" and let it go at that. Professor E.P. Morris, one of the eminent scholars on the fore-and-aft rig, thought the story was a pack of hokum made up after the fact to justify a folk legend. (John Babson in 1860 quotes Cotton Tufts in 1790 quoting some unnamed person in 1791 who says he heard....). In 1927, Morris wrote:

> It is upon the verb "scoons" as the source of "scooner" that the story depends. "And it may be said at once that there never has been any such word in the English language. It is given, of course, in all the dictionaries, but only as quoted from this one passage. The story hangs on "scoons," and "scoons" hangs on the story.
>
> The Oxford Dictionary says that the "scoons" story "looks like an invention." Most certainly it does. "Scooner" was not derived from "scoons," but "scoons" was made up in an attempt, perhaps a humorous attempt, to account for the word "scooner," and the whole story of 1790 is nothing more than a picturesque adornment of the Gloucester tradition.

Yet the word had to have come from somewhere. Though English-language dictionaries cannot pinpoint the origin of the word, perhaps it is because early dictionaries ignored slang, and *scoons* could have been slang. After all, the word *clipper*, as in "clipper ship," is thought to have come from a slang word for fast motion: to clip, to clip along, to run at a fast clip.

Arthur Clark, on the other hand, theorized in his *History of Yachting* (1904) that

schooner came from the Dutch *schoon*. In a Dutch-Latin dictionary of 1599, which he cited as evidence, Clark found that *schoon* was defined as "beautiful or fair or lovely," though it did not have a nautical connotation.

But the Gloucester story really has two parts to it. One has to do with the origin of the word, the other with the invention of the type. Granted, the evidence points toward the development of the schooner rig long before 1721, but the British maritime historian David MacGregor speculates that the supposed coining of the word then may have had nothing to do with the rig. "The 'scooning' of the Gloucester two-master," he wrote in 1982, "may have applied to a new hull-form rather than any alteration of an established rig." Such a theory is worth future exploration, especially since in later years the Gloucester fishing schooner came to be seen as different in character from other working schooners.

There are several schooner subtypes—coasters, fishermen, pilotboats, and yachts—and, to further confuse the matter, there are even sub-subtypes: bay coasters, packets, brickers, traders, stone droghers, Gloucester fishermen, oyster dredgers, and more. Today's windjammers reflect this diversity. Though the Maine cruise-schooner trade is an outgrowth of cargo-carrying under sail, and the tradition it has followed since the 1930s is not much more than a continuation of the time-honored coasting way of life, the schooners that are engaged in the business are not all coasters.

The original coasters of today's windjammer fleet, vessels that at one time actually carried cargo, include the *Stephen Taber*, the *Lewis R. French*, the *Grace Bailey*, and the *Mercantile*. The *Mary Day*, the *Mistress*, and the *Heritage*, though based on the coaster model, never actually carried cargo. The ex-fishermen are the *American Eagle*, the *Isaac H. Evans*, and the *J. & E. Riggin*. The *Timberwind* and the *Roseway* are former pilotboats. The *Nathaniel Bowditch* is a yacht.

But it is not all as simple as it seems. The *French* spent part of her career as a fisherman. The *Roseway* was built as a yacht on fishing-schooner lines and years later was converted to a pilotboat. The *Bowditch* was built as a yacht somewhat on fishing-schooner lines and eventually was converted to a working fisherman. The *Summertime* was built specifically for passenger-carrying, but she was modeled after the old-time pinky schooners, which served as both fishermen and coasters. And, among the fishermen, the *American Eagle* was built for fin fishing out of Gloucester, whereas the *Evans* and *Riggin* were built for oyster dredging on Delaware Bay.

✦

We flew across the bay toward the lower corner of Vinalhaven, the surface of the sea dark blue with patches of purple from the gusty northwest wind. Smoke from a fire on the island was rising a hundred feet or so and blowing horizontally downwind like a ragged pennant. The schooner's rigging, under tremendous strain on the windward side, thrummed and hummed with the force of the breeze. The cook and the galley hand, their afternoon free because supper would be cooked on the beach, came on deck with mugs of coffee and stretched out in the lee of the main cabinhouse. Most of the passengers were similarly situated, tucked here and there—behind the deckhouses, the water casks, the heel of the massive bowsprit—protected from the cold wind and warmed by the sun.

We jibed off Brimstone Island, rounded Saddleback Ledge Lighthouse, the major lighthouse marking the entrance to East Penobscot Bay, and sailed on a broad reach into the Isle au Haut Thorofare, the narrow channel between Isle au Haut on the east and Kimball Island to the west. About halfway through we passed the *Timberwind* coming the other way. She was stepping along like a thoroughbred trotter down the homestretch: all sails set, flags and streamers aflutter, a roiling and frothing wake astern, the picture of speed, grace, and, above all, smartness.

"Will you look at that!" the skipper said with more than a trace of envy. "Enough to bring tears to a glass eyeball."

The *Timberwind* was a beautiful sight, indeed. Built in 1931 as the principal pilotboat of the Portland (Maine) Pilot Association, she had patrolled the outer approaches to Portland Harbor for more than three decades in all types of weather, putting pilots aboard incoming vessels and picking them up from outgoing ones. Retired from service in 1969, she was converted to passenger-carrying in 1971 and based in Rockport, the only windjammer homeported there. At 70 feet on deck, a hair smaller than our schooner, she had an even smaller capacity, as she had been built not for cargo-carrying but as a seagoing home-away-from-home for the Portland pilots.

The best-looking cargo-carrying coasting schooners had a homey handsomeness, an outward appearance that—if vessels have personality (and most sailors say that they do)—suggested honesty, solidity, perseverance, and strength. They were designed by men whose names may not have been household words but who nevertheless knew how to achieve good looks in a vessel within the constraints of great cargo capacity and small crews: John J. Wardwell of Stockton Springs, Camden, and Rockland; John M. Gamage of Rockland; Miles M. Merry and Fred W. Rideout of Bath—all of whom designed some of the most graceful coasters ever built. Their vessels, when seen from a distance, were attractive, yes; pretty, yes; but they tended to be upstaged in the looks department by the pilotboats and their close cousins, the fishing schooners. Built for both speed and sea-worthiness, the pilot and fishing schooners combined the rakishness of the clippers, the elegance of the finest yachts, and the refinement of traditional craft that have been designed for a specific purpose. The first winner of the *America*'s Cup, the lovely schooner-yacht *America*, was built on pilotboat lines.

The pilotboats and fishing schooners, especially the Grand Bankers, were designed by aesthetes. Some of the greatest yacht designers, men who helped set the nautical tastes of the Vanderbilts and the Morgans, the Cabots and the Forbeses, also designed pilot and fishing schooners. Edward Burgess, his son Starling, Dennison Lawlor, B.B. Crownin-shield, Arthur Binney, John Alden. While it is true that Thomas McManus, perhaps the greatest American fishing-schooner designer of all time, was a former fish dealer, it is also true that McManus's eye for a beautiful line and a sweeping curve was as well developed

The grand old *Adventure*, the last of the Gloucester knockabout fishermen, known as the "Queen of the Windjammers" during her heyday in the Maine passenger fleet.

associated with maritime Maine: deep anchorages, clear water, spruce trees growing down to the edge of the sea, granite shores, and unobstructed views of the Camden Hills, the Fox Islands, and the heights of Mount Desert.

Most of the islands of Merchant Row were populated at one time, some relatively heavily, though today they are either empty of human habitation or have a smattering of summer houses. Since the few buildings on the islands are for the most part buried in the woods, the sensation is of emptiness, silence, loneliness, spaciousness, timelessness.

We lowered the yawlboat and the pulling boat into the deep purple water, loaded them with the makings of our evening feast—lobsters, clams, sweet corn, salad, beer, wine, fresh-baked bread—and went ashore to McGlathery, where half the crowd set about gathering driftwood for a fire at the edge of the high-tide line and the other half spread out over the wooded island, exploring the abandoned cellar holes and looking for old graveyard markers. At one time there had been a thriving community on McGlathery, with farmers and fishermen, a church, and a school (in 1873, there were eighteen pupils!), but by the 1880s, the year-round inhabitants were gone; by the turn of the century, the buildings were gone, too. Since then, lobstermen have set up summer camp from time to time, and there have been a few summer rusticators. In 1929, Charles Lindbergh and Anne Morrow supposedly spent part of their honeymoon on the island, in hiding. But since

1955, McGlathery has been owned by a conservationist group, the Friends of Nature, and it has remained uninhabited.

What a meal! We steamed the lobsters and the clams and the corn in great kettles over the driftwood fire. We ate and drank with gusto, our backs to the cool forest and our fronts to the orange and red rays of the sun setting behind the Camden Hills. We picked the shells clean and dumped them into the sea, packed up, loaded up, and headed back to the schooner for hot coffee and, as the skipper had promised, Maine crazy pudding (made with raisins, dates, nutmeg, and more, served warm with cool whipped cream). We sat on deck under the wide open sky and sang songs and counted the meteors shooting across the Milky Way and listened to the wavelets chuckling along the schooner's side. Lights twinkled in the tiny village of Isle au Haut and in the distant town of Stonington.

Then, about ten in the evening, we trooped below to the galley for more dessert, more coffee, more conversation. The skipper was in a storytelling mood, so when someone asked if his father had been a schoonerman, he said, why no, his father had been a farmer a few miles inland from the bay. Then he launched into one of those interlocking shaggy-dog tales for which he was famous.

✦

"My father," the skipper said, "spent his entire life milking cows and pulling rocks out of his fields, but he loved going down to the waterfront to look at the boats. I remember once when he and my mother and me went to Wiscasset, a few miles away. That ride started off late in the summer when we got the new fall Sears, Roebuck catalog. Mother was going through it, ripping out all the bra and panty pictures so I wouldn't see them, and came across a big ad right in the middle, one of those cardboard inserts. It was for something called Quick-Drying Enamel Epoxy Paint. It said, 'Send a dollar for a free sample.'

"Mother couldn't resist. She mailed in her dollar. The free sample came in its own bottle with an applicator brush. It sat there on the kitchen window ledge for about a month, all the while Father grumbling about her wasting a dollar for this free sample. Finally, one Sunday morning, she figured out what to do with it. We had one of those old-fashioned toilets with a varnished wooden seat and a big varnished wooden water tank on the wall with a brass chain. She figured if we painted the seat with the Quick-Drying Enamel Epoxy Paint, it wouldn't look old-fashioned anymore. We'd have a modern toilet. So after we finished doing the chores, Father put the paint on with the applicator brush and that seat was beautiful.

"It said right on the can that the paint dried instantly, wait four hours. So Father said, what the hell, we'll take a ride down to Wiscasset and look at the schooners and by the time we get back, the seat will be dry. Of course, he completely forgot about the hired girl who came in on Sunday afternoons to sterilize the milk cans for the following week.

"Now, Mother was one of those nuts who loved to buy old stuff in antiques stores, and Father was just the opposite. He hated to spend money. So when we got to Wiscasset and parked the old Willys Jeep up the hill and started walking down to the waterfront, Father

Like the *Adventure*, the
Roseway was built in
the famous wooden
shipbuilding town of
Essex, Massachusetts,
the birthplace of most
of the Gloucester
fishing fleet.

was talking to Mother a mile a minute to keep her mind off the antiques stores on Main Street. But he could see the schooners down there and he got so excited about them he lost track of Mother, who hooked off to the left just like that and went right into an antiques store. Father turned around to say something to Mother and she wasn't even there!

"Father said, "God no!" and ran back up the street and into the open door of an antiques shop. When he saw Mother, he knew he was in trouble. She had commenced dickering with the owner on the price of one of those grandfather clocks. It was about nine feet tall, a beautiful thing. In the wink of an eye, before Father could stop them, they settled on a price of fifty dollars. (This was back in the days when antiques were cheap.) Just when Father started to say we didn't need a goddam clock, Mother got into a terrible argument with the owner about delivering the thing. Mother thought the fellow ought to deliver it right away, that day, because she had paid good money for the clock. The owner allowed as how he didn't normally send a truck out to our town before Tuesday, and he would be glad to bring it over about then and not before.

"God, it was awful, the arguing back and forth. Before Father knew what was happening, he was right in the middle of it. He said, "Never mind, I'll take the clock home right now in the Willys Jeep, we've got room in the back," which is what Mother wanted him to say anyway. She roped him right into it. So Father, who was kind of slow when it came to catching on to Mother's maneuverings, so to speak, muckled ahold of the clock and threw it onto his back and started to walk up the hill to the Willys Jeep, instead of bringing the Jeep down.

"Wiscasset has kind of a steep hill and Father was huffing and puffing and he was taking up most of the sidewalk, him and this bulky old grandfather clock. Well, lo and behold, wouldn't you know it, here comes Archie, the town drunk, with a wicked hangover from the night before. Archie's coming the other way and he's taking up most of the sidewalk, weaving back and forth. By gorry, they met and Father said, 'Oh my god,' and he kind of dodged over to one side, and of course Archie, who was kind of seeing double, dodged to the same side. They met head-on with a jolt and both went over backward right on their asses. That grandfather's clock went straight up in the air and came down with a tremendous crash and little brass gears rolled all the way to the waterfront.

"Father was some angry. He turned to Archie and said, 'For Christ's sake, Archie, why don't you watch where the hell you're going?'

"Archie looked at my father and said, 'Goddamn it, Willard, why don't you wear a wristwatch like everyone else?'"

The crowd in the galley erupted into laughter. The cook, who had heard this story at least a hundred times, started beating on a pan. She had tears in her eyes.

"But there's more to it!" the skipper yelled above the din. "We still had that Quick-Drying Enamel Epoxy Paint back at the farmhouse."

"Oh, no!" the cook said. "Not that!"

"Oh, yes," the skipper said, pouring himself another mug of black coffee and settling back, with a beatific look on his face.

"We picked up the pieces of the clock and shoved them into the back of the Willys Jeep and, four or five hours after we had left, got back to the house. Father shut off the engine, expecting silence, but what we heard instead was all sorts of screaming and caterwauling coming from the upstairs bathroom. Mother says, 'Holy cow, the hired girl. I forgot to tell her about the free sample.' So Mother ran upstairs and looked in the keyhole of the bathroom door, which was locked, and said, 'Yup, she's stuck fast.'

"We got a ladder from out in the barn and put it up against the outside of the house and Father and I climbed in the bathroom window. We opened the door for Mother. Father and I just stood there snickering. Mother came in and smacked me upside the head and said it ain't funny and commenced pulling and yanking on the hired girl. But she still was stuck fast to the seat. Then Father got out a wrench and took the seat off to get her free, but even then she couldn't straighten up. She was in hysterics. She was hunched over with this thing glued to her backside. Mother went around back and hung on and Father grabbed the hired girl by the shoulders and started pulling and twisting. They didn't get anywhere. She was just screaming louder. So they decided to take her over to Doc Skillins. He was our family doctor from way back and would surely know what to do.

"So we put the hired girl in back of the Willys Jeep and put a horse blanket right over her and Father drove lickety-split right into town. We trundled her out, kind of bent over under this blanket, crying and whimpering all the time. There was one of those know-it-all receptionists at the front desk—you know, the type that wants to know next of kin and all that first and what's wrong with you later. So we gave her the particulars and then she said, 'What seems to be the trouble here?' Father whipped off the horse blanket. She looked kind of shocked and rang the bell and one of those smart-alecky interns showed up.

"The smart-alecky intern looked the hired girl over and said, with buckets of self-importance, 'I can take care of this,' and he and Father opened the double doors of the examination room so they could get her in. They got her up on the examination table on all fours, the toilet seat glued onto her backside looking right at us. I'm snickering and Mother's smacking me on the side of the head and Father's hanging onto the girl's shoulders and the smart-alecky intern's not doing any better than Mother. Finally he decides he's got to go upstairs and get old Doc Skillins.

"In a few minutes, the old doc himself comes down. Well, he was the general practitioner in our town for a century and a half and a wise old man if ever there was one, and he looked the part. Great white beard, big hooked pipe, tweed jacket with elbow patches. There we were all lined up by the doorway—the receptionist, the smart-alecky intern, Father, Mother, me with a sore head.

"That smart-alecky intern turned to the doctor and said with a knowing air, 'Doctor, did you ever see anything like that in your entire life?'

"Doc Skillins looked at the intern, looked around at the receptionist, Father, Mother, me. Then he looked at the girl. Then he took his pipe out of his mouth and said, "'Why yes, I have, but never with a frame around it before.'"

IX *Souvenirs of Another Age*

Yes, one of the brightest gems in New England weather is the dazzling uncertainty of it. There is only one thing certain about it. You are certain there is going to be plenty of it—a perfect grand review. But you never can tell which end of the procession is going to move first.

—Samuel L. Clemens

Friday morning came like a hangover. The cheerful islands of the day before; the bright, glinting, chortling sea; the singing wind in the rigging—all had been replaced by dripping, drizzling, cold, gray, raw, wet, dull, damp, sodden murk, enough to drive most of the passengers back into their bunks a few seconds after they emerged. Even the crew, normally stirring by six o'clock (the cook an hour earlier), was late getting started.

"What's the rush?" the mate asked, sprawled on a wooden crate in a corner of the galley, drinking black coffee. "The skipper hates to sail in weather like this. We'll be here for quite a while if I'm not mistaken."

He wasn't. The NOAA marine weather report had a grim edge, though the droning meteorologist speculated that the low rain clouds of the morning would give way to higher clouds with intermittent showers in the afternoon. The skipper didn't even bother to listen to the whole report. He got to the part about quarter- to half-mile visibility with light winds and drizzle and snapped off the radio. "Relax," he said to those passengers who were up. "Have a nice, slow breakfast, snooze a bit afterward, read a book, take it easy. We'll stay put if it's all the same to you."

I helped myself to a bowl of hot oatmeal and a mug of coffee and idled away an hour or so in the galley, reading here and there in a copy of *Islands of the Mid-Maine Coast*, which I had borrowed from the ship's library. More genealogy than history, drier than scorched toast, it still managed, in flashes of insight, to convey the romance of the outer reaches of the coast and the loneliness of a region that had risen with an industrial maritime culture and had fallen when it died.

"With the gradual decline and final termination of the quarrying industry," wrote the author, Charles McLane, "Crotch Island was left devastated, with large sections of it uninhabitable. The millpond where David Thurlow had built his schooners and brigs had been cut to a third of its original size by discarded slag, the tops of the haughty granite hills were lopped off, and the island was abandoned by its inhabitants. Only one of the

"I filled a thermos with coffee, grabbed a couple of dough-nuts, pulled on my boots and foul-weather pants, and borrowed the skipper's pulling boat."

homes standing at the turn of the century still stands. A haunting beauty nonetheless pervades the island. An abandoned quarry on an island keeps a dignity usually lost by its counterpart ashore, where realtors are too quick to hide the scars and start afresh."

Nothing if not a romantic, I filled a thermos with coffee, grabbed a couple of doughnuts, pulled on my boots and foulweather pants and jacket, and borrowed the skipper's pulling boat. Crotch Island was only a couple of miles from McGlathery. Rain or no rain, I was looking for haunting beauty. Besides, I needed the exercise.

It was a dismal pull. The bottom edges of the clouds, only a few hundred feet above me, were ragged and gray. The water was the color of concrete. The islands looked as if they had been painted with a wash of used crankcase oil. Those objects with color—the gilded nameboard on the schooner receding in my little Whitehall's wake, the orange life jackets in the bottom of the boat, my yellow waterproof trousers, a red plastic container on the shore of one of the islands—seemed to scream with intensity in comparison with the dullish blear of everything else. There was no wind to speak of; the only movement in the air was a fine, misty rain that fell without cease. The handles of the oars and everything else were slippery from the wet.

I rowed through Merchant Row. My route was around the north of Wreck Island, between George Head and St. Helena islands, and straight to the northwest toward Crotch Island. Except for me, the only objects in motion on the water to the visible horizon were a few sea ducks diving for a midmorning snack. The little schooner *Mistress* was holed up in a cove on Wreck Island, and the low, sleek, black-hulled *J. & E. Riggin* was lying off St. Helena. Both had awnings rigged below their booms to provide on-deck shelter from the rain, but no one on either vessel was taking advantage of the protection. I rowed unnoticed past both of them.

There was machinery running on the southeast side of Crotch Island and a barge was tied to some pilings, so I stayed in the boat and rowed up into the crotch, the narrow east-west inlet that gives the island its name. It was like taking a water route through a junk-yard. There was rusting metal on the shore, and just in from the edge were broken-down buildings and the remains of cranes and heavy lifting equipment. I beached the boat on the southern side of the inlet, tied the painter to a mooring stake left from the old schooner days, and pushed my way uphill through the puckerbrush.

The sight from the top was enough to give one pause. The top half of about a third of the island looked as if it had been blown away by a bomb blast. There were sheer cliffs in what had once been a gentle hillside, a couple of huge, deep holes filled with water, several others that weren't, and piles of rubble strewn across the half-naked landscape. A good part of this island, the very foundations of it, had been cut into blocks of various size, some big, some small, and shipped off to cities all across the country. Over the years, several quarrying companies, major operations employing hundreds of men, hacked away at Crotch; the tonnage shipped out is incalculable. Imagine the number of schooners, the number of schoonerloads, it took to move it all! How many did it take to haul the tons and tons of stone for the Mount Holyoke Dam on the Connecticut River? The Museum of Fine Arts in Boston? The Pilgrim Monument in Provincetown, Massachusetts?

The most spectacular schoonerload out of Crotch Island came in 1914, when the John L. Goss Corporation shipped a 50-ton granite bowl aboard the three-masted schooner *Susan W. Pickering* for Tarrytown, New York. A replica of a 1576 bowl in the gardens of the Royal Palace in Florence, Italy, it was destined for the Rockefeller estate in Pocantico Hills. (The Rockefellers were serious buyers of Maine granite. Stone from Crotch Island was also used in the construction of Rockefeller Center in New York City.) The bowl, more than 20 feet in diameter and three feet deep, was turned from a 225-ton block of flawless granite using machinery especially designed for the operation. Seventy wooden rollers, several block-and-tackles, and a portable steam engine, securely anchored to the ground, were required to move the bowl from the turning site to a loading wharf and then into the hold of the *Pickering*.

I'm not sure the quarries on Crotch Island could be called hauntingly beautiful—at least not on a day that made the most beautiful objects, such as the schooners *J. & E. Riggin* and *Mistress*, which I could see from where I stood, look downright dowdy—but the island and its evidence of superhuman activity did have a certain lonely elegance. Like the stone walls running through the new stands of trees that have grown up on much of Maine's coastal farmland, the imploding wooden hulks along the coast, and the rotting ferry pens on the Woolwich shore of the Kennebec across from Bath, the Crotch Island quarries are in their own way a monument to one of the several ways of life that existed on the coast

"I stayed in the boat and rowed up into the crotch, the narrow east-west inlet that gives the island its name. It was like taking a water route through a junkyard."

Camden, primarily a yacht harbor today, was once a down-and-dirty coasting-schooner port. Remnants of that era are a few rotting timbers of the *Annie F. Kimball*, lying in a tiny backwater near the head of the harbor.

of Maine not that long ago. Yet these ways have been very nearly obliterated by the rising tide of modern times. Unofficial and unmarked, they are better than the monuments that are official and marked because they tell you nothing. They force you to understand them yourself. If you are successful, you can achieve a sense of satisfaction that no bronze historical plaque or homogeneous, condensed "interpretive" brochure can ever provide.

In Camden, on the eastern side of the inner harbor, a stone wharf belonging to Wayfarer Marine—one of the larger yacht yards on the coast—fronts a tiny cove with no name, the only backwater left in a harbor that has otherwise been developed beyond development. The people of Camden and the passengers of the cruise schooners homeported in that town have a clear view from the head of the harbor right into the cove. To most of them, at low tide, it is nothing more than a sea of mud studded with bits of rusting chain, old tires, broken bottles, and other odds and ends of nautical detritus. Few, other than potential waterfront real-estate developers looking for a few more feet of frontage to set up more businesses to cadge more money from the tourists, pay it any mind.

But to the maritime buffs, the romantics (and there are more of them than you would think) who know the history of some obscure corners of the coast better than they know the name of the capital of Vermont, the little cove with no name is almost a shrine. For right in the middle of it is what appears to be a shapeless mound of wood, a random collection of broken timbers that seem to have been thrown there—out of sight, out of mind. The pile of timbers contains the remains of the *Annie F. Kimball*, built more than

100 years ago, the first vessel owned by Captain Frank Swift as a cruise schooner. You can, if you are of a mind, wade out into the muck at low tide, reach down through the seaweed and sucking mud, and pull out a wooden treenail that once held the *Kimball*'s planking against her frames.

There are hulks at sites like that all along the coast, some known only by the cognoscenti, others right out there in the open for everyone to see. The most famous, of course—because you have to be asleep to miss them—are the *Hesper* and the *Luther Little*, the two huge schooners lying on the shore of the Sheepscot River in Wiscasset. You drive northeast on Route 1 into the town, past the shops and the restaurants, Red's Eats on the left and a hardware store on the right, cross the railroad tracks, come onto the bridge, look to the right, and bango! there they are. Spars akimbo, decks caved in, rigging trailing into the water, holes in the sides. On the one hand, a sight of utmost desolation; on the other, a vision of the past that is dignified in its indignity, if you know what I mean.

The *Hesper* and the *Luther Little*, to the untutored eye, look like sister ships, and in some ways they are. Both were four-masted wooden schooners built during the shipping boom of World War I; both were constructed in Somerset, Massachusetts, in yards that were virtually in sight of each other. (The *Hesper* was built by Crowninshield Shipbuilding in 1918, the *Luther Little* by Reed Brothers in 1917.) Both were designed as bulk carriers for long-distance coastal voyaging, not harbor-hopping like the bay coasters. But each had separate owners and careers unrelated to Wiscasset until they joined each other in the summer of 1932, locked together in a decline that continues to this day.

Built for emergency World War I commerce, the *Hesper* and the *Luther Little* were launched so close to the end of the war that they were doomed from the start. Yes, they hauled lumber and coal up and down the eastern seaboard—the *Hesper* even made a few transatlantic crossings with coal to Portugal—but, like the rest of their sisters, they couldn't come close to earning the profits anticipated by their owners because of the postwar shipping depression. By the mid-1920s, both vessels, as majestic as they may have been, were just about played out in the economic sense. By the end of the decade, they were laid up in anticipation of a shipping upturn that, as fate would have it, wouldn't come for another ten years, until the onset of another world war. By 1932, their owners, who could see only the Great Depression of the present and nothing of a windfall from a conflict to come, could not or would not make good on various claims against the vessels, which therefore were auctioned off in partial settlement. Those were the days when big, four-masted schooners, including all their accoutrements—boats, donkey engines, blocks, anchors, miles of rigging, galley equipment, skipper's stateroom furnishings, the works—went for a tad more than a song, but not much more. The *Hesper*, pride of the northeast coast, brought her creditors six hundred dollars.

Those were also the days when entrepreneurs, operating on a shoestring, with just about zero seagoing sensibility, were coming up with a scheme a minute for such then-useless (in a maritime sense) vessels. It was the time of the schooner-dance hall, schooner-tearoom, schooner-gift shop, schooner-bordello. Frank Winter, who bought the *Hesper*

One of the saddest sights
on the coast of Maine—the
mortal remains of the four-
masted schooners *Hesper*
and *Luther Little* next to
the bridge in Wiscasset.

and the *Luther Little*, didn't have plans quite as crass as that, but they were just as unrealistic. He hoped that his schooners-on-the-cheap would secure the maritime link of a mini transportation route that included a narrow-gauge railroad terminating in the village of Wiscasset. It is an axiom of the nautical world, however, that laid-up wooden vessels deteriorate faster than those in use. Long before the various parts of Winter's plan were in place (in truth, they never were; the railroad was scrapped for the war effort), the schooners had become unseaworthy. As it turned out, the last voyage of the *Hesper* and the *Luther Little* came at the end of the hawser of the tugboat that towed them up the Sheepscot River to Wiscasset from Portland.

✦

One of the peculiar characteristics of lumber schooners, when compared to the schooners of the current windjammer fleet, is the presence of lumber ports in their bows. These openings were specially designed for loading horizontally into the vessel long balks of timber that otherwise would not fit through the conventional hatches in the main deck. Openings as large as these bow ports were a menace to the watertight integrity of a ship at sea, so once the schooner was loaded, the ports were closed and dogged down tightly, and the seams were carefully caulked.

Lumber was one of the principal cargoes of the coasting schooners, large and small, especially during the declining years of the sailing coasters, when the only way to compete with steam and motor ships, which could deliver their cargoes on time, according to schedule, was to carry loads with flexible delivery schedules. Lumber schooners were packed from keelson to deckbeams with timber, the hatches were battened down, and usually, to increase capacity, a deckload was laid on top. Some loads were so high that the helmsman had difficulty seeing over the top; if he couldn't see at all, a lookout atop the pile would shout steering instructions to the man at the wheel.

Schooners that carried high deckloads on a regular basis were fitted with a special pinrail in the shrouds for securing the halyards and other running rigging, as the normal pinrail would have been obscured by the lumber. Also, they sometimes had what was known as a "lumber reef" in the sails, below the first regular reef, which allowed the boom to clear the top of the load.

Deckloads were common on hay schooners as well. In the days before the truck and the automobile, hay for horses was a major coastal commodity, shipped on small- to medium-size schooners from saltwater farms to cities such as Portland, Boston, and Providence, where immense quantities were required year round. Baled hay was packed in a vessel's hold, piled high on deck, and covered with a canvas tarp to shed rain and spray. An unprotected deckload of hay could quickly become waterlogged in a storm, which could raise the center of gravity of the vessel so much that it could become unstable and capsize. Such a tragedy befell the hay vessel *Royal George*. Caught off Monhegan Island by a thunderstorm with winds so powerful that the tarpaulin was blown away and the hay became soaked, she capsized and foundered.

The crew of a lumber schooner with a deckload didn't have waterlogging of the cargo to consider, but they did have to worry about the consequences of ice pileup in the winter and a shifting pile of lumber at any time of the year. "[One] afternoon," Biff Bowker wrote about a coasting voyage in the 1930s, "we passed through a mile-square patch of heaving, surging new lumber which shortly before had been the deckload of some other vessel bound our way....It was not unusual for a schooner with her decks piled high with lumber to have such an accident. Sometimes when a vessel was overwhelmed by the seas, or perhaps hove down on her side by a shifting deckload, it would be decided by the master to cut the lashings in order to bring the vessel up and so lighten her that she could fight safely through a storm."

Even if she should be knocked down by a shifting deckload or spring a leak and fill with water, a lumber schooner seldom sank, as she could always float on her cargo. Consequently, many coasting schooners that had been employed carrying other cargoes were put into the lumber trade near the end of their useful lives, because a leaky hull could always be offset by the buoyancy of the cargo. During the last, dying days of the sailing coasters, there were so many derelict schooner hulks in the Atlantic—dismasted, filled with water, just barely awash, unsinkable yet unsailable, abandoned by their crews, menaces to navigation—that the U.S. Coast Guard sent out search-and-destroy patrols. The Coast Guard cutters carried demolition experts, who boarded the vessels and fit dynamite charges with timed detonators to blow the hulls apart.

The smaller vessels in the lumber trade were employed carrying light loads, mostly intrastate, from the small-time sawmills way up the obscure tidal creeks and rivers. The larger vessels, the huge multimasted coasters built specifically with such bulk cargoes in mind, were used in interstate commerce all along the eastern seaboard, down in the Caribbean, and even for transatlantic passages. In a variation on the coals-to-Newcastle theme, huge quantities of lumber were carried by schooner from southern to northern ports, including Maine, at the same time large amounts of Maine timber were shipped in the other direction. This sounds stranger than it really was, for the shipments from the North tended toward softwoods such as white pine, spruce, and fir, while those from the South were longleaf yellow pine (also known as Southern yellow pine or hard pine), oak, and the tropical hardwoods of the Caribbean.

Perhaps because Southern yellow pine was seen in the North as exotic and Eastern white pine as local and therefore mundane, many homes built in Maine at the end of the nineteenth century were of the imported species. Many of the houses in the major shipbuilding towns such as Thomaston, Rockland, Camden, Belfast, and Searsport were constructed with hard pine, for both framing and interior woodwork. Even in Bangor, once one of the greatest lumber-exporting towns in Maine, many houses were built of hard pine imported from the South. So, too, were wharves, granaries, bridges, railroad ties, and ships, though not because of any notions of fashion. Rather, Southern yellow pine was more practical. Lying somewhere on the scale between pure hardwood and soft-wood, it was stronger and more durable than the softwoods, yet lighter in weight than the hardwoods. Most of the big schooners built in Maine during the latter part of the nineteenth century and the beginning of the twentieth were constructed of Southern yellow pine. Well, not totally. Decks were usually of white pine, masts of fir, and the paneling in the skipper's cabin, as befitted a shipmaster of means, was usually of such hardwoods as walnut, cherry, mahogany, and bird's-eye maple.

Consider this for a moment: Schooners were built in Maine to transport lumber from Maine to the southward. Hard pine and Southern oak was shipped north to Maine in schooners to build the necessary schooners. As more schooners were needed to ship the lumber from the South, more lumber was shipped to the North to build the schooners, so more schooners were required to be built....

Lumber imported from the South to Maine went to the ports near where the lumber would be used, so the major shipbuilding towns were visited regularly by bulk lumber schooners. Before the turn of the century, the largest ports for exporting lumber out of the state were Bangor (at the head of navigation on the Penobscot River) and Stockton Springs (near the top of Penobscot Bay). As the logging industry had shifted its focus to eastern Maine when the virgin central forests had been cut over, the down-east ports of Machias, Calais, and others now became the centers of commerce.

In the nineteenth century, lumber was the lure on the Penobscot River. "Always in memory most closely associated with vessels in the lumber trade and with the river front of Bangor in the old days," wrote George Wasson in *Sailing Days on the Penobscot*, "was the fragrant smell of immense lumber piles, and the acute, aromatic odor of cedar shingles." Logs were driven down the river from the interior of Maine to the mills of Bangor, and the lumber sawn from them was shipped all over the world. Millions of board feet. In fact, a shipment of slightly more than a million board feet once went out of Bangor on a single vessel, the *S. E. Smith*, which departed for Liverpool, England, on July 14, 1862, no doubt staggering under the load.

"Looking down Penobscot Bay on a fine summer day," wrote Wasson, "after a period of bad weather in which Bangor-bound coasters had collected in various harbors, there was often to be seen a marine picture which, taken as a whole, was not to be equalled on the entire coast....Up the Bay they sped in almost endless procession....The westering sun lighted up with warm glow each swelling sail and the flashing wings of gulls added touches of a vision of marine activity never to be forgotten and of which the present generation can have but the slightest conception."

Indeed, you would never know about all this by looking down the river and out into the bay today. In 1873, the *List of United States Merchant Vessels* showed two ships, seven barks, thirty-one brigs, and 131 schooners and sloops, most employed in the lumber trade, and at least a dozen tugs and steamers homeported in Bangor alone. Today there are none, and there are few reminders that they ever existed. Gone are the wharves, the slipways, the sailmakers, the chandleries, the coalyards, the sparmakers, the smithies, the shipyards on both sides of the river. Gone are the huge sawmills, the lumberyards, the shingle mills, the log booms, and the immense piles of sawdust.

"Looking down
Penobscot Bay on
a fine summer
day...there was
often to be seen
a marine picture
which, taken as a
whole, was not to
be equalled on
the entire coast."

The *Hesper* and the *Luther Little* aren't the only visible schooner hulks on the coast of Maine—just the most accessible. The four-master *Edna M. McKnight*, built in Camden in 1918, and the five-master *Courtney C. Houck* of 1913 lie in Mill Cove, behind the town of Boothbay Harbor. The *Mary F. Barrett* of 1901 lies in Robinhood Cove, Georgetown. The five-master *Gardiner G. Deering* of 1903 lies on the other side of the harbor from Castine in West Brooksville (she was burned to the waterline to celebrate the Fourth of July in 1930). The *Cora F. Cressy* of 1902, built in Bath's famous Percy & Small Shipyard, had post-coasting stints as Levaggi's Showboat in Boston and as a lobster pound in Maine, and now lies in Medomak as a breakwater.

Those are the schooner hulks. The schooner bones, less visible, are more numerous. At low tide in nearly every harbor, you can find pieces of keel, deadwood, framing, and planking half-buried in the mud. They are all that is left of vessels, wrecked or no longer economical, that were run up on the shore and abandoned.

Even on McGlathery Island, off which our schooner was safely anchored, there are bones—a few timbers, visible at extreme low tide, of the three-master *Wawenock*, which in 1929 hit a ledge off the island and drifted onto the southeastern shore facing Gooseberry Island and Isle au Haut. Unlike other wrecks and hulks, however, only a very small portion was left to rot. Unauthorized wreckers descended like locusts and stripped the ship of her fittings, fastenings, woodwork, and timbers. In a week, all that remained were some frames and the schooner's keel.

Old schooners today, no matter their condition, are treated with substantially more respect. In fact, perhaps as the result of the recent rise in preservation consciousness around the country, they are approached with reverence. Just as certain businesses and groups have recognized that it is good economics to preserve and restore old buildings for new uses (i.e., you can make money), others with a maritime frame of mind have discovered the same to be true for old vessels. The preservationists' buzz phrase, which issues from the lips of supporters of the National Trust for Historic Preservation and other similar institutions, is "adaptive reuse." Adapt an old cotton mill and reuse it for elderly housing, a church for condominiums, a boiler room for a restaurant, a train station for a shopping mall, an oyster dredger for a cruise schooner.

Actually, the cruise-schooner business had been practicing the principle of adaptive reuse long before the term was coined, never mind made a foundation of urban redevelopment. During the period from the 1930s to the 1960s—when the wrecking ball was in full swing ashore and the National Trust still thought a building with historic significance was one in which George Washington spent a night—several coasters, fishing vessels, and pilotboats were converted to cruise schooners. But by the end of that approximately thirty-year span, the stock of adaptable vessels, those of sound hull, was just about used up. Waterfront observers came to the conclusion that all the old schooners that could become passenger vessels had become passenger schooners. Any new wooden vessels introduced to the fleet would have to be built for the purpose from scratch, and that would be a rare occurrence, as the cost of construction in the modern era was so high and the wooden shipbuilding skills were so low and the essential materials—oak, ironwork, ship spikes, blocks, etc.—were so scarce.

The argument seemed logical enough to the older generation, whose members had become accustomed to an unlimited number of hulls to adaptively reuse but who failed to consider the resourcefulness of a new crowd of younger would-be schoonermen. No sound hulls? the newcomers said. What the hell, we'll go to work on the unsound ones, the vessels that a few decades ago would have been driven onto a mudflat to be digested by the worms. This wasn't adaptation or "fixing up" or repair or anything like that. This was in effect total reconstruction. When the new crowd was finished with the rebuilding of a vessel, it was difficult to find any of the old vessel's original parts.

The first schooner in today's cruise-schooner fleet to be given this treatment was the 65-foot centerboarder *Isaac H. Evans*, built in 1886 at Mauricetown, New Jersey, as the oyster dredger *Boyd N. Shepard*. She had a checkered career on Delaware Bay, having been rebuilt a number of times, including once after a fire in 1954 and again after sinking in the winter of 1966. Converted to power in 1946, with the addition of a pilothouse, she was hardly recognizable as a schooner when Doug and Linda Lee bought her in 1971 for a few thousand dollars. The Lees brought the *Evans* north to Bath, Maine, where they hauled her out on the banks of the Kennebec River and, over a couple of years, rebuilt her. During the course of the reconstruction, which involved gutting the interior, tearing out all the rotten frames and planking and replacing them with new, and fitting brand-new passenger accommodations, they invested close to $50,000 and a total of about 18,500 hours of labor.

The pioneers of the windjammer trade, people like Captains Frank Swift, Frederick Guild, Jim Nisbet, and Havilah Hawkins, would never have considered such an expenditure of time and money on a rotten corpse. Theirs was the frame of mind of the old school, which held that once an old wooden vessel was used up, it was finished and that was that. Yet the Lees proved with the *Evans* that dying schooners could be revived, and, by their example, they encouraged others to give it a try. In the space of a few years, Captains David and Susan Allen rebuilt the 89-foot centerboarder *J. & E. Riggin* of 1927, another Delaware Bay oyster dredger that had been converted to power (she also served as a mackerel fisherman off Long Island); and Captain John Foss rebuilt the 64-foot *Lewis R. French* of 1871, a former coasting schooner that is now the oldest vessel in the windjammer fleet.

Now, even cruise schooners that in the old days would have been considered far too old and decrepit to continue in the fleet and would have been sent to the boneyard are being completely rebuilt. In recent years, Captains Ken and Ellen Barnes reconstructed the *Stephen Taber* and Captain Ray Williamson did the same to the *Mercantile* and the *Mattie*, now known as the *Grace Bailey*. Major portions of all three vessels were almost hacked and shoveled into a pile of broken, rotten timbers and either burned in the shop stove to keep the shipwrights warm during the winter or trucked to the local dump.

Why go to the trouble? Why rebuild an old schooner, especially one like the *Mattie*—

"Why go to the trouble? Why rebuild an old schooner?" The *Mercantile*, built on Deer Isle in 1916.

which was in such poor shape when reconstruction began that there were very, very few original timbers in her when the job was finished—when for not much more money and time, you could build a brand-new vessel? Why not take off her lines, draw up construction plans, pull her up on the shore and burn her or tow her out to some lonely spot of ocean off Matinicus Island and pull the plug, and then rent shop space down on the Rockland waterfront and build a replica?

The answer is that the *Mattie* is the *Mattie*, and a replica of the *Mattie* is not. Even though it is true that George Washington's ax—the one that is so old the handle has been replaced eight times and the head three—is no longer, in a technical sense, the same ax used to chop down the cherry tree, it is nevertheless a lineal descendant of the original. A replica of that ax, one built as close to the original specifications as possible, though not necessarily cheap, is still an imitation. The *Mattie* that emerged from the rebuilding shed after major reconstruction in 1989 and 1990 had some or all new frames, planking, deckbeams, decking, deadwood, fastenings, transom, knees, and who-knows-what-all, but she still had pieces of original structure melded into the new, and, more important, had the aura of the old *Mattie*, the peculiarities, the atmosphere, the qualities that set her apart from all other schooners. She also had the old *Mattie*'s original name, the *Grace Bailey*.

The *Mattie*, after all, has been sailing in the Maine windjammer fleet since 1939, when she was chartered by Captain Frank Swift (before he purchased her a year later), making her the longest runner in the fleet. She was built in 1882 as the *Grace Bailey* in Patchogue, New York, for the West Indies lumber trade. Rebuilt in 1906 and given a new name, she went on to New Haven, Connecticut, to become an oyster buy boat, then was bought by Captain Herbert Black of South Brooksville, Maine, with money he received from the U.S. government to replace his schooner *Oakwoods* after she had been rammed and sunk by a submarine in Buzzards Bay. Under Captain Black and then Captain William Shepard of Deer Isle (who eventually sold her to Captain Swift), the *Mattie* carried general cargo along the New England coast. She even carried stone from Crotch Island to New York City.

✦

I picked up a rusty iron quarryman's wedge and put it in my pocket as a souvenir of Crotch Island. (Stone was quarried by drilling holes along a natural seam, driving in iron wedges with a sledge, and then splitting out a block of granite.) The clouds were as low as they had been all morning, and the misty rain continued, but there was a sense, a barely perceptible hint, of a coming moderation in the weather. I scrambled down the hill to the little Whitehall pulling boat, bailed out most of the rainwater, and pushed off. Over in Stonington, just across the Thorofare from where I emerged from the crotch of the island, the schooner *Nathaniel Bowditch*, looking more like an old-style traditional yacht than a passenger vessel, was motoring into the anchorage to pick up lobsters from the fishermen's co-op. Down among the islands of Merchant Row, a half dozen or so lobsterboats were working the traps. Our schooner swung to her anchor off McGlathery, the long green streamer at the head of the topmast folding and unfolding in a gentling breeze. There was a hoot from the mailboat running down to Isle au Haut, and a shout from the schooner: "C'mon, Pete. Soup's on!"

X Sailors and Islands

The seaman considers himself more red-blooded than the man who stays at home to live a humdrum existence on the farm, in a factory or an office. He feels that his life is in a broader world than that of a preacher who lives with his books, and as he looks at the sea around him, he is able to ask himself questions that he knows no man can answer. He knows that a man washed overboard is more apt to be saved if he swims and forgets to pray than if he prays and forgets to swim. Of course, if he uses both methods and is saved, he can take his choice of which to credit.

—Francis E. Bowker, *Blue Water Coaster*

Life slowed to a crawl. The rain continued through lunch, past lunch, into the early afternoon. Boredom set in. Several of the passengers went on deck to watch a fellow with a Folbot—a collapsible, canvas-on-wooden-frame kayak packed in a soft-sided suitcase—unfold his craft, snap it together, launch it over the side, and paddle it around the schooner a few times in the rain. The maneuver was about as exciting to watch as a wallpaper hanger at work. ("Like watching moisture condense on my eyeglasses," as one wag with bifocals put it.) Those smart enough to come in out of the rain hung around the main cabin or the galley, reading and kibitzing.

About one-thirty in the afternoon, the skipper came down to the galley, where the mate and I were studying a chart of Penobscot Bay. He poured himself what was probably his tenth cup of coffee of the day and paced around while he drank, antsy as a third-grader waiting for the recess bell to ring.

"I can't take it anymore," he finally said. "This sitting here at anchor has gone on too long.

"What do you think?" he said to the mate. "Get underway, rain or no rain? We could pick up a fair breeze to North Haven. At least anchor off a real town, go ashore. They've got a general store there, you know."

Nobody said a word.

"Good idea," the skipper said. "We're going."

The skipper's word was law, even on a schooner where most of the occupants paid for the privilege to be aboard, rather than the other way around, so we pulled on our foulweather gear—the cook, the galley hand, the mate, a handful of passengers—and trooped on deck to set the sails and haul the anchor. Any hope of staying dry ended when we set the main. As we pulled on the halyards, one gang on one side of the deck with the peak halyard, another gang on the other side with the throat, buckets of water trapped

"He was happiest at sea, or ashore working in a boatshop or a shipyard." Glen Brooks, first mate of the *Isaac H. Evans*, standing on the main boom.

in the folds of the heavy canvas sail poured down on our heads. Same thing with the foresail, but since it was slightly smaller, we got slightly less wet, which was no consolation at all. I had water inside my pockets and several inches in the bottom of my boots.

The wind and the current, though both light, were such that the schooner lay with her head facing into the passage between Round Island and McGlathery. Without enough room to fall off to port or starboard and sail out of there, the skipper decided to back her down under sail, an operation that is simple for the experienced and potentially disastrous for those who are not. He sent a deck crew forward under the direction of the mate to back the foresail and hold it in position with a preventer—a length of line rigged to keep the sail from swinging—while he sheeted in the mainsail until it was as flat as he could get it, the main boom lying fore-and-aft along the centerline of the vessel. When the anchor was pulled free from the bottom with the windlass, the pressure from the wind on the forward side of the backed foresail caused the schooner to sail slowly backward. As momentum increased, the skipper shifted the wheel so the stern slid to port, then he nodded to the mate to cast off the preventer, and, as the bow of the vessel came across the wind, set the headsails. The schooner slowly, gently, pivoted on her centerboard until she had turned 180 degrees from the direction she had initially been headed. We trimmed the sheets and sailed around the eastern side of St. Helena Island and out into East Penobscot Bay.

In our time, most yachtsmen in sailboats half the size of our schooner would have difficulty even imagining how they would undertake such a maneuver in tight quarters without power, never mind doing it. In the heyday of the coasters, the skippers of the huge multimasters did that and more without much more thought than a driver of an automobile equipped with power steering would give to parallel parking on a city street. John T. Rowland described his experience in the 1920s aboard the four-masted schooner *C.C. Mengel, Jr.*, a vessel without auxiliary power, approximately three times as long as ours, and infinitely more awkward:

> One day when the vessel was lying in the stream of a swift tidal river at Hillsboro, Nova Scotia, it was desired to bring her in and berth her at a dock about three hundred yards away. I asked the Skipper if he wanted a tug.
>
> "Reckon not," he replied, without offering any explanation. I could not imagine how he would manage it.
>
> We were lying a short distance upstream from the dock, and the tide was running ebb a good four knots. The anchor had a long scope out. First the Donkey-engine man raised a whopping head of steam and broke out the hook on the run. Then the Skipper put his wheel over and held the vessel at an angle of about thirty degrees to the stream. With the current rushing past her sides, she crabbed sidewise towards the dock. At the end, he had to head her up into the current until she lost headway and drifted gently back to her berth.

But that was only half of the story. After loading a consignment of gypsum at the dock, the *C.C. Mengel, Jr.* took advantage of an ebbing tide to make her way down the river to the Bay of Fundy—*backward*!

Rowland wrote:

When the ebb tide got running strong (she was still heading upstream), we cast off the bow line and let her head cant out; then, as she started moving away from the dock, the other lines were let go in turn. The big schooner with 1,400 tons of rock in her hold eased out towards the middle of the river by her own inertia, drifting backwards scarcely at all. There we dropped an anchor at short stay and let it drag on the bottom. This gave the schooner steerageway as she drifted slowly down river, stern foremost.

Backward down a river to the Bay of Fundy in a ship more than 200 feet long, and this was business as usual!

The old coastermen had to face adversity on a daily basis. They were adept at converting bad situations to good and making do when normal men in normal circumstances would rather not. Sailing the largest wooden ships without auxiliary power, with, at best, a yawlboat powered by a balky engine; strapped for operating capital in the latter days of sail; undermanned, setting out with greenhorn crews; facing leaking hulls, short schedules, lee shores, and all the rest; getting underway on a tidal river without benefit of a tugboat—they met each situation as it came as if it were nothing more than another task in a long string to be performed in a day's work, and when you get right down to it, that is what it was. What men! What sailors!

Yet it is all too simplistic to suggest that they don't make them the way they used to and to become sentimental about the lost skills of seamen past. Yesterday's sailors may have included men of maritime wizardry like the skipper of the *C.C. Mengel, Jr.*, but not all of them were so skilled. The next skipper of the *Mengel* drove the vessel in light airs and a calm sea onto a cay in the Caribbean and she became a total loss. Today's sailors may have an easier time of it due to the advances of the last fifty years or so, but if they were in the shoes of the old coastermen, some, just as in the old days, would rise to the same occasions and others, also just as in the old days, would botch the job.

No matter the era, the crews aboard sailing ships have always been a mixed bag of the skilled and the unskilled, the professionals, the romantics, and the incompetents, though it is safe to say that the quality of the sailors —their abilities, the length of their experience, their reliability—for the most part depended on the health of the shipping business in general. During a period of ascendancy, such as the mid- to late nineteenth century, when the clipper ships and later the Down Easters dominated the ocean, there was ample opportunity for those who wished to follow the sea. Waterfronts were crowded with men familiar with seafaring—men who could hand, reef, steer, box a compass, handle the ship's boat, maintain a wooden vessel, stand watch, navigate, make a longsplice, repair a torn sail, and practice the rest of the arts of the sailor. Shipowners had their pick of the best.

During periods of decline, however, such as the years following World War I in the sailing coaster fleet, there was little opportunity for seamen to practice their trade. More ships were laid up or scrapped than were in service, and good berths were few and far between. The skilled sailors, seeing the handwriting on the wall, drifted over to the steam and motor ships or found better-paying jobs ashore. The owners of sailing coasters found themselves employing unskilled sailors or greenhorn landsmen. hired at the last minute to fill out the crew.

The schooner owners were caught in a mess partially of their own making and partially caused by economic forces beyond their ability to control. As powered vessels made their inroads on the cargoes traditionally carried by the sailing coasters. the owners of the sailing coasters tried to meet the competition by cutting costs. The most obvious ways to accomplish the latter were to reduce the size of the crews by the introduction of laborsaving devices—the most notable being the donkey engine used to raise the sails. pump the bilges. and haul the anchor—and to pay substandard wages. At first. fewer berths meant more competition for those berths remaining. but later. as the skilled seamen. discouraged by the decline of the sailing fleet. turned to alternative work. it meant far fewer sailors in the labor pool and relatively unskilled ones at that. The substandard wages only hastened the change. The average deckhand became overworked and underpaid.

Captain Jim Sharp of the *Adventure*.

"The business of coasting was an exceedingly hard way of life." wrote William H. Bunting. "The question of how badly the coastal sailor was 'used' must be judged in relation to one's notion as to the balance between free will and economic compulsion. and—most importantly—in comparison with the prevailing standards. There is no question but that from the standpoint of conditions today. life aboard even the finest schooner was frequently dangerous and uncomfortable. and that the sailor received little pay for his labors. But low wages and dangerous working conditions were characteristics of many trades ashore. and had always prevailed at sea."

However perceived. prevailing conditions or exploitation. by the late 1920s the largest schooners were crewed by a handful of men who were paid a pittance by the standards of today's merchant mariners. even when the dollar has been adjusted for inflation. A four-master after World War I. for example. could get by with about a dozen men. including the skipper. on about fifty dollars a day for the entire crew. The skipper. the mate. and the donkeyman (the engineer) were often the only experienced sailors on board. Skippers like that of the *C.C. Mengel, Jr.* had to be able to work their way out of the most difficult situations on their own. since their crews were small and usually on the green side. The smallest schooners. the bay coasters and traders. were having their own difficult times. They were struggling to get by with the proverbial man. boy. and a dog. Eventually. by the end of the 1930s. all the coastermen were unemployed—that is. all except those who sailed with the windjammer fleet.

✷

About a half hour after we set sail. the rain stopped and the mist cleared out and the wind—typical for a weather change in the early fall—began to blow hard from the westnorthwest. ("Aha!" the skipper said. "Got the jump on it this time.") With the improvement in the weather. the skipper changed his course from the direction of the Fox Islands Thorofare to that of Hurricane Sound at the southern end of Vinalhaven. but halfway across East Penobscot Bay, he changed his mind again. We tacked and headed up the bay on a close reach, since we would otherwise have to beat into a strong wind through the sound, not a pleasant prospect in close quarters.

Windjammer skippers would have you believe that we would sail for a week footloose and fancy-free without schedule or specific destination, going with the wind, anchoring for the night wherever we might happen to find ourselves at the moment. In a normal week without threat of a storm, if you ask the skipper in the morning where he will be at night, you'll get an answer like, "Oh, I don't know. Maybe here, maybe there. Wherever the wind takes us." Such a vagueness sounds seductive and romantic to a passenger eager to get away from it all, but the truth is that the skipper is always thinking ahead, no matter what he might be saying. At the beginning of the week, a skipper won't go anywhere from which he can't be certain of returning at the end of the week. For example, he won't sail with the summer's prevailing winds much farther downeast than Schoodic Point because of the uncertainties of the beat back. So, too, he won't beat to the westward at the beginning of the week if there is even a suggestion in the long-range forecast of easterlies at the end of the week.

Near the end of a week of cruising the Maine coast, a windjammer skipper will begin to think about positioning himself for the last night, since the goal of the final day of sailing, Saturday, is to arrive in the schooner's homeport sometime before noon. The favorite Friday-night anchorages, therefore, are a straight-shot, half-day sail to home, no matter what direction the wind may be blowing. Pulpit Harbor, North Haven, Gilkey Harbor, sometimes Rockport if home is Camden or Rockland, or Camden if it is Rockland or Rockport. Windjammers have been known to spend the night as far away as the Barred Islands or down the Muscle Ridge in Tenants Harbor, but only if the prospects of a fair wind are virtually guaranteed.

Our skipper wasn't letting on where he would cast the anchor on this last night—he would wait first to see where the other schooners would congregate, as he looked for company but not too much of it—but our slant up the bay seemed to point toward Pulpit or Gilkey Harbor. Probably the former, since with a northwesterly, we could make a long board back down the bay straight for it in the late afternoon. Our destination seemed so obvious, in fact, that the mate failed to interest anyone in a harbor pool—a betting pool on where we would spend the night. Instead, he established an anchor pool, with each entrant putting down a dollar and picking the hour, minute, and second when the anchor would splash down. In no time at all, he had a roll of twenty-some-odd dollar bills in his pocket.

The mate was, simply stated, a traditional sailing-vessel enthusiast. He was happiest at sea, or ashore working in a boatshop or a shipyard, but he had his standards. No fiberglass or steel boats, no yachts if he could help it; fishing vessels, perhaps, but above all else schooners. He had crewed aboard wooden vessels in Maine; on the Hudson River aboard the sloop *Clearwater*, operated by an environmentalist group; on the Chesapeake in the skipjack fleet, the last of the sailing fishing vessels operating in North America; in the Caribbean aboard a charter schooner; and in California on a sail-training vessel, a replica of a revenue cutter of the mid-nineteenth century. He was a professional sailor at a time when the common perception was that such a class of people no longer existed. He had worked in several different boatshops building small craft, and had had been a carpenter in the building of the schooners *John F. Leavitt* at Wallace's in Thomaston and *Heritage* at the North End Shipyard in Rockland, and the rebuilding of the *Stephen Taber*, the *American Eagle*, the *Mercantile*, and the *Mattie*. In the winter, when our schooner was laid up at a wharf over by the old O'Hara fish plant in Rockland, he rented a one-room apartment over a neighborhood grocery store and kept his shipwright's tools in the trunk of his car, a 1978 Datsun that looked as if it had been attacked by a gang of bikers with chains and sledgehammers. When he shaved, which wasn't very often, he used a boar's-hair brush and a porcelain cup with a broken handle, and he ate breakfast in greasy-spoon restaurants with truck drivers and electricians and carpenters.

The mate was a romantic, a nineteenth-century man trapped, to his great regret, in the twentieth century. He came out of the back-to-the-land movement of urbanites and suburbanites who fled to the north country in the late 1960s, early 1970s, and took up residence in old farms and cabins and found nobility in simple work and simple pleasures. He was from a middle-class neighborhood outside New York, yet he looked and acted like a down-home Mainer, a salt of the everlasting sea. He was what is known on the coast of Maine as a schooner bum: the type who would rather plait sennit (make fancy ropework), muck out bilges, caulk seams, and eat yellow-eye beans out of a can than get a white-collar job in an office and live in a suburban house with trimmed shrubbery and drive a Saab around the gentrified Old Port District of Portland. He would have loved to have worked in a shipping warehouse in the Old Port back in the 1880s, for example, when it was simply the Port of Portland, and would have happily spent several years at the turn of the century on a small coaster carrying barrel staves to the westward, and coal, feed grain, and salt for the fishing fleet to the eastward—but he was born too late for all that.

Though today's schooner bums share certain characteristics with yesterday's coaster-men—a fascination with the sea; a restless, wandering nature; a romantic bent tempered by the reality of hard work for low wages—they are in many ways quite different. The crew members on cruise schooners today tend to give the impression of being educated, literate, well-spoken men and women who, if they changed their hairstyles and their clothes, would be as qualified to engage in any middle- to upper-echelon white-collar occupation in modern America as they are to work as deckhands, mates, cooks, galley assistants, boat carpenters, caulkers, and riggers. Our mate didn't go to college, but he could have. Many of his colleagues did. In fact, most of the skippers in the fleet went to college, and several had careers in more conventional fields before they became professional sailors.

By contrast, the coaster crews of the earlier part of this century tended to come from the working class; most of the men (there were no women other than, occasionally, the wife or daughter of a skipper) were itinerant laborers. The permanent members of a schooner

Crewing on a schooner can
be a risky business. A mate
in the rigging works to clear
the topsail.

crew amounted to, at most, the skipper, the mate, and the cook. The rest of the men, the deck and galley hands, were signed on for a single voyage and discharged as soon as the vessel returned to port. When the schooner was ready to put to sea once more, the owners signed on a new crew, usually men who had never sailed on the vessel before. In the late nineteenth and early twentieth centuries, these itinerant laborers were at least professional seaman, but as the coasting cargo-schooner age limped along into oblivion in the 1920s and 1930s, and the professional seaman went into steam and motor ships or fell by the wayside, schooner crews were made up of whomever the owner or owner's agent could cadge together. Many coasting schooners put to sea with sailors who were that in name alone; they didn't know the mainsheet from a boltrope—and, what's more, they didn't care.

There was, however, a class of young men who went into schooners in the 1920s and 1930s of a different sort than the more typical down-and-out waterfront drifter. They were bright and eager romantics who went to college and sought adventure in sailing vessels afterward, or didn't go to college because they couldn't wait for the adventure to begin. Young men such as John Leavitt, Biff Bowker, and John Rowland jumped from land to sea out of the sheer, unadulterated romance of coastal sail and made no bones about it. They were so enthusiastic about the experience that they went on to write articles and books about their time during the declining days of sail, and at the very least indirectly influenced those who followed them into the Maine passenger schooners. They saw themselves in romantic terms as swashbuckling coastermen, the last of an era, yet at the same time recognized the reality of the situation: They were performing all of the chores of the sailor, but they, like today's passenger-schooner sailors, were of a new order, rubbing shoulders with the remnants of the old but not of it. Biff Bowker touched on the matter in describing life on board the four-masted schooner *Alvena* in the 1930s:

"The four young men in *Alvena*'s forecastle were not city-bred men drawn from the hustle and bustle," Bowker wrote in *Blue Water Coaster*. "All of us were from small towns, yet tempered to the pace of urban life by frequent contact with the busy cities. Aboard *Alvena* we had settled down, with little complaint, to conditions our grandfathers had known. Outwardly we seemed a regular crew of schooner sailors, but a short conversation would have exposed our differences to a veteran sailor."

We sailed up the bay past the eastern entrance of the Fox Islands Thorofare and the western entrance to the Deer Island Thorofare, the 'longshore of Deer Isle on our starboard side. We ranged along a string of islands on our port side, passing one after another like beads in a necklace. Calderwood, Sheep, and Bald islands; the Porcupines, Eagle, and Butter—the latter two at one time the most heavily populated of the small islands in mid–Penobscot Bay and now as empty as the least populated. There were visitors today on Eagle, however; we could see what seemed to be little stick figures in brightly colored jackets by the Eagle Island lighthouse, and a couple of small motorboats pulled

"We trimmed the sheets and
sailed around the eastern side
of St. Helena Island and out
into East Penobscot Bay."

Eagle Island Light, with the Camden Hills in the distance. At one time there were almost a hundred year-round residents on Eagle Island. Now there are none.

up on the shore of the cove tucked behind the point.

In these times of rampant population growth in most parts of the country, especially the Northeast, we tend to think of the coast, especially Maine's, as having been underpopulated—virtually empty—in the old days, and being a heaving morass of development now. In our mind's eye, we see every inch of habitable coastline covered with recently built vacation homes and motels and condominiums, with more under construction and even more in the planning stages. When we think of islands, we think of Long Island in New York and Block Island off Rhode Island, Martha's Vineyard and Nantucket off Cape Cod, mostly open land at the turn of the century and now suburbanized and holiday-resorted to the nth degree. Yet the islands of Penobscot Bay—even the large, accessible ones such as Islesboro, North Haven, Vinalhaven, and Deer Isle—are nowhere near as populated now as they were fifty, seventy-five, one hundred years ago.

Eagle Island, for example, was inhabited continuously from at least 1810 until 1979, when the last permanent resident departed. It was an island of farmers, fishermen, boatbuilders, and lighthouse keepers, and, at its height near the end of the nineteenth century, was home to between fifty and a hundred people, most of whom were related to one another (the primary family was the Quinns, seconded by the Howards and the Carvers). At one time there was a small hotel, Quinn House, which operated during the summer months from the turn of the century until 1931. Guests arrived by steamer or passenger launch from Rockland and North Haven.

The islands of the bay, as remote as they may seem, especially when viewed from the deck of a schooner, have always been a major part of the economy of mid-coast Maine, their populations rising and falling with the strength of the economy ashore and the occupations of their inhabitants paralleling those on the mainland. The saltwater farms on the islands died out within a decade or two of those on the mainland; the old-fashioned summer-residence hotels like Quinn House—where rusticators came for weeks, even months—closed about the same time as their old-style competitors across the water. Quarrying, fishing, ship- and boatbuilding, logging—all of these industries came and went in step with the rest of the state.

Few of the inhabited islands, all of them probably, could ever be seen as romantic microcosms—isolated, self-sustaining, self-perpetuating societies in which a person could bury himself and live only on food produced and goods manufactured there. Like the coastal mainland, which depended on water transportation almost exclusively until the early decades of this century, and relied on it to a considerable extent afterward, they were served continuously by schooners, sloops, steamers, and launches bringing supplies, manufactured goods, and visitors, and hauling away produce, fish, logs, lumber, and stone. As much as the islanders liked to think of themselves as something apart from the rest of Maine, they were very much a part of the state.

When the railroads and then the highways came to be the primary transportation systems in Maine after World War I, and water transportation went into a decline from which it has never recovered; when the construction trades no longer looked to granite as a fundamental building material; when the mid-coast lime industry died out and the kilns no longer needed cordwood from the islands for fuel; when the paper plants were built in inland Maine and looked to local forests for pulpwood; when refrigerated transportation permitted the shipment of fresh produce from more productive farms in the midwestern and western parts of the country; when vacationers came to prefer motels they could reach by automobile rather than hotels accessible only by boat—the island economies in a general sense were strangled and the residents moved ashore, returning only as occasional or summer visitors.

The fishermen remained on some of the islands, especially the larger ones that were served by ferries and fuel tankers. (Fuel became most important to the fishing industry when the fishermen switched from sail to power craft in the early decades of the century; those who didn't, who stayed with sailing or rowing boats, ultimately had to give it up, as their operations had become economically uncompetitive.) Vinalhaven, Deer Isle, and Matinicus are the principal fishing islands of the bay these days. Carvers Harbor on Vinalhaven and Stonington on Deer Isle are served by an extensive network of fish dealers, suppliers, boatyards, and fishermen's cooperatives, and have dependable means of getting the fish and lobsters to market—by road and the Deer Isle bridge from Stonington and by the Maine State Ferry Service from Carvers Harbor. There are fishermen on some of the smaller islands, too, but most of them come for the summer, living in camps or aboard their boats and returning to their homes on the larger islands or on the mainland for the winter.

Like elsewhere in the state and New England in general, the islands of Maine are given over increasingly to summer vacationers, but nowhere to the degree that they are elsewhere, like Martha's Vineyard, Nantucket, and Block Island. The major summer islands of Penobscot Bay—those with integral economies depending on people "from away"—are Islesboro and North Haven. Vinalhaven, Deer Isle, Monhegan, and a handful of others are shared to a greater or lesser extent between the fishermen and the summer visitors (to the delight of the latter, who come as much for the local color as the weather, and the tolerance, at best, of the former). The small islands such as Eagle, Butter, Great Spruce Head, Lime, Mark, Hog, Pickering, and hundreds more ranging from less than an acre to a few hundred acres in size are either uninhabited in both summer and winter or have a few summer houses and camps and nothing else. Most are privately owned, either by an individual or a family, or piecemeal by several owners. The state owns some; conservation groups, such as the Maine Coast Heritage Trust, the Nature Conservancy, and the Friends of Nature, own others.

They are magnificent islands with an overall collective sameness of rockbound shore, rounded profile, and forest cover of spruce, fir, hemlock, and other conifers. But to us on our schooner, there were enough variations among them to keep the view interesting as we made our way up the bay in a moderately strong northwesterly. High, low, studded with fields and clearings, treeless, populated, unpopulated, pink granite, gray granite, jagged ledges, steep cliffs, smooth stones, sand beaches, shingled beaches, deep coves, grass green, spruce blue, birch white—everything you could wish for and more.

✦

We were just north of Fiddle Head Island near the bell buoy that marks the western entrance to Eggemoggin Reach when the skipper, seeing a schooner turning the corner off The Triangles just inside the Reach, called the mate back to the wheel.

"Set the topsails," he said, "and then put together a gang of sheet trimmers who won't mind focusing their attention on the job for an hour or so. We're going to have a race." The schooner tacking her way out of the Reach was the *Heritage*, and this time our skipper had not been caught by surprise.

We hove to for a few minutes by the bell buoy, waiting for the *Heritage* to make her way down. Then, as she drew near, all sails set, a long pennant streaming from her foretopmast, the American flag fluttering from her maintopmast, our skipper spun the wheel so we gained way again and then tacked. Canvas flogged briefly as the mate and his crew handled the sheets. In a flash we were headed back down the bay, neck and neck, rail to rail, with the *Heritage*.

"Pulpit Harbor!" the skipper yelled across the narrow gap separating the two schooners. There was white froth at the bow of the *Heritage*; a roiling wake trailed off astern. "First to anchor stands the loser to supper."

"You're on," Captain Lee shouted back. "You might as well start cooking!"

Both schooners charged for the passage between Beach and Horse Head islands on one

Pulpit Harbor on the island of North Haven. Pulpit Rock lies right in the middle of the mouth. Vinalhaven, the next large island (at top in photo), is separated from North Haven by the Fox Islands Thorofare, one of the major passages on the coast of Maine.

side and Great Spruce Head and Little Spruce Head on the other. When both schooners emerged and corrected courses for North Haven, a straight shot in clear water, the *Heritage*—a larger vessel with more sail area and a longer waterline—was slightly ahead. She held her lead and gained a little more, enough so we could read the name and hailing port on her transom. But this was Penobscot Bay and it was late afternoon, and as each minute passed, the wind, true to form, lost more of its strength. The *Heritage*, a heavier, wider, and deeper vessel than ours, sailed better in strong winds, while ours, though hardly a thoroughbred racer, was a shade faster in light winds. We were gaining on the competition off Egg Rock Ledge and dead even as we entered the harbor channel between Pulpit Rock and the eastern shore of the entrance, both vessels almost within touching distance, streaming along on a broad reach straight for the back shore of the harbor. We were so close, in fact, that I could see the lines of concentration on Captain Lee's brow and clearly hear his instructions to the crew.

Just when it seemed that both schooners would be dancing partners forever, hard aground on the harbor shore, our skipper, who held the windward edge, shouted to Captain Lee, "I'm going to turn to starboard!" and Captain Lee replied, "Fine, then I'll turn to port and jibe." And he did and we did. Our schooner turned, quick as a cat, and shot up into the wind. The *Heritage*, jibing, turned a wider, slower arc; while Captain Lee was still waiting for the way to come off his vessel, our skipper was signaling to the mate to drop the hook. A cheer erupted from the crowd on our deck, followed by a single shout of victory from the winner of the anchor pool. Later, Captain Lee came across in his yawlboat with a large basket covered with a red-and-white-checked tablecloth, and he and our skipper sat on the cabinhouse, their backs to the mainmast, and ate their supper as the sun set in screaming pinks and oranges behind the Camden Hills.

Our supper was an all-out feast. Roast beef, gravy, green peas, baked potatoes, sourdough rolls, salad, cherry and peach pies still warm from the woodstove oven, hot coffee, and tea, the table livened with laughter and storytelling. Following the meal, as was traditional on our schooner on Friday night, the male passengers kicked the women out of the galley, including the cook and the galley assistant, and washed the dishes and pans and cleaned the tables and benches and swabbed the galley floor and sang songs and drank beer. Then we grabbed a bucket of crushed ice, some heavy cream, sliced peaches, rock salt, dishes, spoons, and an old-fashioned hand-cranked ice cream machine and went on deck.

The galley assistant got out her guitar and sang about lost love and long voyages, and then the skipper stood up by the rail and told one of his patented stories. Much later, when most of the passengers had gone below to their bunks or were stretched out in sleeping bags on the roof of the main cabinhouse, I took a long, slow row around the harbor in the light of the waning moon. From deep in a cove about half a mile away, our schooner and the *Heritage*, their anchor lights lit, were the picture of a past I had never seen—yet here I was in its presence. I felt very fortunate.

"She held her lead and gained a little more, enough so we could read the name and hailing port on her transom."

"He and our skipper
sat on the cabinhouse,
their backs to the
mainmast, and ate
their supper as the sun
set in screaming pinks
and oranges behind
the Camden Hills."

XI *Another Link in the Chain*

The caulking mallet striking against its iron creates a piercing, ringing sound which carries for a great distance and lets the world know that something is going on, that work is being accomplished, that ships are taking form.
—Dana Story, *Frame-Up!*

The door to the North End Shipyard in Rockland, Maine, was slightly ajar, despite the lingering cold of an early spring day. I pushed it open without knocking and stepped into a large, square room with exposed rafters and an ancient wooden floor that undulated like the ocean on a calm day. Directly in front of me was a huge maroon shipsaw with portable rollers, but the machine was quiet, as was the entire shop; the polished surface of the steel table was proof enough of the miles of heavy oak that had been cut by its blade.

To my right, in one corner, was a blackened forge surrounded with anvils and tongs, quenching buckets, hammers, bags of soft coal. There was a welding torch with acetylene and oxygen tanks, and along the south wall was a long workbench littered with cutters and nippers, vises and grinders. Nearby were a lathe and a drill press, and underfoot were chunks of scrap steel and curls of shining metal. Four sooty welders' masks rested on a shelf.

At the back of the room, to the left of the shipsaw, was a thickness planer half-buried by coarse wood chips; on the north wall was a bank of switches and transformers. By my left hand was an even larger planer, and through a door to the side was the granddaddy of them all—a huge, black, baroque machine fitted with rollers and guides and adjusting wheels, a working antique, a planer that finished lumber on all four sides with a single pass. On the walls hung recently galvanized ironwork for a large sailing vessel. The floor was buried in sawdust. I could smell the mustiness of damp ashes, the freshness of cedar and pine, the sharpness of green oak.

I crossed the room and pulled aside a gray canvas curtain that had been roughly cut from an old rope-bound sail. I entered another room, a joiner's shop with a long workbench running the length of the north wall. On the bench were tools of every description—planes and drills, saws and clamps; some in boxes, others left lying where they had been used. Underneath were even more. A film of fine dust covered everything, even the posters and calendars tacked to the wall. Through the cobwebbed windows I could see a huge

The coasting schooner *Heritage*, the newest schooner in the fleet.

steambox and firetube boiler, the latter topped with a stovepipe and a brass steam whistle, and beyond that was a small cove and a wharf topped with three cedar-shingled timber-frame buildings connected in an L shape.

Directly ahead of me, leading to a storage loft and a small apartment, was a staircase, behind which stood a matched pair of bandsaws and a table saw. In the southeast corner were shelves of paints and oils, thinners and solvents, tars and proprietary compounds, and along the side of the staircase were bins of fastenings, mostly galvanized—bolts and nuts, screws, nails, drift pins. On the floor was a large shipwright's chest, packed to the brim with worn but obviously cared-for hand tools. To my right was a homemade wood-stove built from odd pieces of steel and iron bolted and welded together; the stovepipe, in its long traverse to the chimney, was supported with scraps of baling wire. Caulking tools hung on the wall.

A faded sign hung over a door: Ship's Store & Office. In the office, a rolltop desk stood open, its pigeonholes crammed with papers and canceled checks; on top was a ledger, surrounded by ripped-open envelopes and hastily penciled notes. Half models and framed photographs of ships hung on the paneled walls; well-thumbed catalogs from chandleries and industrial suppliers were jammed in a bookcase. A black cast-iron Victorian stove rested on a rough brick hearth; the fire within settled a bit, and the pleasant scent of woodsmoke permeated the room.

Against the wall was a small drafting table with a rectangular sketchbook open on its surface. Drawn carefully in profile was a nineteenth-century two-masted coasting schooner. The caption said *Heritage*.

November 28, 1979

Last winter I spent a month putting all the ideas on the drawing board. Everything that a Penobscot Bay windjammer should have and big enough to go anywhere. The result, three sets of lines later, countless hours, lots of money spent (Linda says $17,000 to date, yet we haven't even finished the lofting floor), is our new schooner—93 tons, 93 feet long by 24 feet wide by 8 feet draft, with a centerboard, two topmasts, main topsail, and flying jib. It will be beautiful but such a long way away. We'll get there somehow.

We are trying to do this without killing ourselves. We plan this as a five-year project. The idea is to stop when we run out of money each year. Fat chance. Hopefully we can contain ourselves so we don't go and borrow too much too early and get into trouble....

—from Captain Douglas Lee's journal

The shop crew was outside, tearing down a temporary sheet-plastic shed that had sheltered the *Heritage* and obscured her from full view since her keel was laid in early 1980. Captain John Foss was up on the roof with a few helpers, freeing the trusses with a chainsaw, while Captain Douglas Lee operated a mobile crane that lifted each piece clear and lowered it to the ground.

The air was electric with excitement, for the end of a monumental effort was in sight. Next week a team of house movers was to jack up the schooner and shift her sideways onto

"Everything that a Penobscot Bay windjammer should have and big enough to go anywhere." The *Heritage*.

the railway where she was to be launched; two weeks after that, she would slide into Rockland Harbor. One year of thinking, one year of planning, three years of building, and a new wooden schooner would be afloat, despite the scuttlebutt that said nobody in this day and age could afford to build such a vessel, that said nobody possessed the skills anymore for wooden construction on such a scale, that said nobody would be foolish enough to invest so much in an endeavor that would return so little.

Ever since Doug and Linda Lee graduated from college, where they met and were married in the late 1960s, they had been rebuilding old schooners and sailing them in the passenger trade. Doug started out with the *Richard Robbins*, a tired New Jersey oyster dredger, assisting with her reconstruction and then sailing aboard her as galley hand, mate, and finally skipper. He and Linda, with the part-time assistance of John Foss and other volunteers, rebuilt the former Delaware Bay oyster dredger *Isaac H. Evans*, sailing her as a husband-and-wife team. He and Linda and John Foss in partnership rebuilt the down-east cargo schooner *Lewis R. French*, which Foss then skippered in the passenger trade. All was done on a shoestring, on an almost capital-less, pay-as-you-go, learn-how-when-you-must basis. They ate hot dogs and macaroni and hung their hats in the cheapest housing to save money, and when the money ran out, they took jobs, any jobs, to get started again. They waited on table, clerked in shops, repaired small machinery, did odd jobs, shoveled fish meal, and did anything else to make money so they could do the only thing they really wanted to do—sail their own coasting schooner in the passenger trade.

December 28, 1979
We started lofting on the 4th of December. Got the lines faired by the 15th of December—12 days with numerous distractions to fair up the lines. Then picking off and drawing in the frames (40 of them), the centerboard, and the transom—12 more days with numerous distractions....

January 8, 1980
Today is an historic occasion. This is the first day we actually cut into a piece of wood that will be in the schooner. Today we cut and planed the stem. We flipped over the timber with a forklift, since it is too heavy for us to horse around with cant dogs....

January 12, 1980
Today the first two pieces of wood were joined together. We fastened the first piece of gammon knee to the stem....

January 23, 1980
We haven't any more keel stock to work with. Brooks Mill has had trouble with their generator, and they don't really have any logs big enough for the 10 $\frac{1}{2}$" x 12 $\frac{1}{2}$" x 20' keel piece. Out of desperation we cut all the futtocks for frame 1. What a job! I tried to cut both sides at once, laying out all the pieces at the same time. Sure enough, it got so confusing we made two pieces for the same spot....

—from Captain Douglas Lee's journal

Much is made of so-called Yankee ingenuity, that fabled quality of New Englanders, especially down-easters, to do what they want, when they want, the way they want. Social commentators of late have suggested that this trait is a thing of the past, corrupted from the populace by the insidious lure of modern comforts. This may be true, but the Lees and Foss know nothing of it. You would be hard pressed to find a more independent lot; in fact, if you hung around Rockland long enough, you would swear you had discovered the mother lode.

Doug and Linda and John not only wanted their own schooners to sail up and down the coast, they also wanted to have their own self-contained shipyard, where they could haul and maintain their own vessels, and embark and disembark their own passengers. Part of it was simply the desire to be totally in charge of their own affairs, but part was atavistic—the ambition to own a nineteenth-century shipyard to match their nineteenth-century vessels and their nineteenth-century frame of mind. The modern way to achieve the latter has been to become affiliated with a museum and rely on government and foundation grants to re-create and restore a "historic" shipyard; but, of course, you don't get much independence that way.

So just when the Lees and Foss appeared to have it made—they owned the *Isaac H. Evans*, they were building their reputations in the passenger-schooner marketplace, they had income instead of outflow—they leased, then bought outright a parcel of land on the Rockland waterfront with a couple of tumbledown buildings and weeds in the yard—an industrial site with a fish-rendering plant next door, a steel fabrication plant out front, and a seaweed-processing complex across the water. It wasn't particularly expensive, but it was enough to send them back to adventurous housing and macaroni and hot-dog suppers.

January 31, 1980
   Today I went over to Brooks Mill. There was Karl himself just starting to saw one of the 20' x 12 1/2" x 10 1/2" pieces of keel. Still need two more like it. I ended up as Karl's helper....

February 2, 1980
   It is amazing to me, the amount of logs we have looked over just to get keel pieces, and we still don't have them....The chances are some slim that you can look at a log and actually get what you want out of it.

February 8, 1980
   Condemned the second 18' x 10" x 12" timber we have gotten from Brooks. A big, bad spot six feet from the top....

February 12, 1980
   Yesterday John and I went over to Brooks Mill. I picked out what I guessed was the best log of the lot. None looked particularly inviting, with badly split butts and big rotten-

looking knots. We cut four feet off the butt, leaving eighteen-plus feet. The butt seemed to clear up and really looked pretty good. Karl spent almost two hours sawing that log, and it looks great. What a surprise! I convinced Karl to move in another piece—a huge one this time that started out 26 feet long. We cut six feet off the butt to find good wood, and two feet off the top. Got two 12 x 12s, one 10-footer, and one 8-footer, the forward and after fillers, below the keel. Now we have everything to build the keel....

—from Captain Douglas Lee's journal

The Lees and Foss founded the North End Shipyard, where outside users could rent space and lease tools and do their own work; Doug, Linda, and John, who wanted to be independent and free from others' demands, would work on their own projects. It was there that the *Lewis R. French* was rebuilt, a couple of new yawlboats were built, and a sandbagger was restored; Dave and Sue Allen rebuilt the schooner *J. & E. Riggin*; Ken and Ellen Barnes rebuilt the *Stephen Taber* and converted the sardine carrier *Pauline*; John Foss converted the old fishing schooner *American Eagle*; and other owners hauled their vessels for major repairs.

Just setting up the yard itself was a major undertaking. The buildings had to be strengthened and modified, a marine railway for hauling vessels had to be built, industrial-quality tools had to be purchased—and rebuilt if they were secondhand, which most of them were. There were chimneys to rebuild, permits to be obtained, and wiring and plumbing to install.

Most projects were done from scratch. To save money, the shingles for the main shop building were made with an old shingle-sawing machine. Big jobs were tackled as if they were small, and small jobs were done while the glue was setting up or between supper and the evening news. What are the time periods we are talking about here? 1971–73, rebuild the *Isaac H. Evans*; 1974–76, set up the yard and rebuild the *Lewis R. French*; 1977, think about the future.

February 24, 1980, Sunday
Day off, don't you know. Spent the morning planing the sides of the deadwood. In the afternoon I finished both tail feathers...;

February 25, 1980
Started building the framing floor in the afternoon. Since the *Heritage* is a centerboard vessel, the framing floor is built straddling the keel where the centerboard will be. This was planned when we put up the building; there isn't room enough ahead of the vessel to put the floor. All the full frames can be made and stood up. Then the half frames for the bow and stern can be made and stored off to the side until we're ready for them. The half frames in way of the centerboard are made last, then the framing floor will be torn up....

February 26, 1980
We finished building the framing floor by lunch, then started lining out frame 30,

which is the first full frame of the after section….At about 3 p.m. we suddenly realized there wasn't any six-inch stock for making the timberheads. So John and I rushed over to Brooks's. Karl was sawing oak at the time, but he agreed to saw out several pieces of six-inch stuff. It arrived around 5 p.m. That's service!

March 1, 1980

People started arriving before lunch, and by 2:30 over 150 people had come to see the Frame-Up. At 3:01 we stood her up and slid her under the keelson. When it was all the way back I said, "OK, that's it." And a tremendous cheer went up….

April 1, 1980

Quit work on the *Heritage* for the winter, started fitting out the *Isaac H. Evans* for the summer.

—from Captain Douglas Lee's journal

By 1977, things were starting to fall into place at the North End Shipyard. The *Lewis R. French*, owned in partnership by the Lees and Foss, had joined the fleet, skippered by Foss. There were plenty of small- and medium-size jobs to be done in the off-season: work on the rundown houses they had just bought, maintain their vessels, improve the shipyard, but nothing time-consumingly, mind-paralyzingly, finances-back-to-zero big.

For a while there, things started to look up: When John went out to the front of his house to renail a loose clapboard, his hammer went right through the rotten wood, back of which was a rotten stud, below which was a rotten sill, over which rested rotten floor joists. John happily jacked up the house, tore everything out, laid down a new sill, and threw in a bunch of new joists. But let's not kid ourselves: It was a house, not a boat.

Meanwhile, Doug and Linda Lee were thinking about a bigger schooner. They talked about more passenger-carrying capacity and room for the children they hoped to raise and other practical considerations, but the true motivation was probably tied up in the North End Shipyard itself. After all, anyone who goes to the trouble of setting up a shipyard must have in mind the building of ships.

There comes a time in every boat-rebuilder's life when he starts to think about new construction, when he comes to the realization that more or less the same amount of work goes into the rebuilding of someone else's idea of what a boat should be as would go into his idea of the same thing. Why rebuild someone else's dream when you can build your own from scratch? The Lees had, indeed, considered finding another old hull, a bigger one, and rebuilding it, but they rejected the idea after taking stock of what they had—the tools, the facilities, the knowledge of supply sources, the skills developed after years of full-time experience. They knew that if they didn't build a new schooner now, they might never, and they knew that John Foss was as itchy to try a truly big, challenging project as they were and would help them.

End of October [1980]

   Resumed work on the *Heritage*.

November 12. 1980

   Glen and I spent a good part of the day working on the centerboard log. which is over three feet at the butt and 30-plus feet long. It had been a beautiful oak tree obscuring someone's view of the water. It cost me $500 plus cartage and had been soaking in the cove since July. The game plan is to rough it out with the chainsaw mill. When the lift truck tried to move it, the weight of the log broke the frame of the truck. A bad morning....

November 14. 1980

   Rich Ford showed up with a helper and the "Alaskan Mill." We set up a four-inch piece of garboard stock as a straightedge guide along the top of the log. and they made their first cut. Took three and a half hours....

November 15. 1980

   We had a real early blizzard on Tuesday, which of course covered the framing pile. Got things shoveled off over the next few days. Late Friday afternoon we started tearing up the framing floor....

December 10. 1980

   Finished framing today. All frames. including the transom. transom side pieces, and the knightheads. are in. Essentially a phase is over. that of the backbone and framing. Tomorrow a new phase begins—planking....

                                        —from Captain Douglas Lee's journal

   Doug and Linda Lee met John Foss back around 1972. when John was in the Coast Guard down in Boston and used to hang around the schooner fleet in Camden and Rockland during his time off duty. He knew a career in the Coast Guard wasn't for him. that working on schooners was, and—given the same background (Maine upbringing. college education. fanatical interest in boats inherited from similarly obsessed fathers)— he and Doug hit it off the first time they met. John spent the rest of his Coast Guard weekends working on the *Isaac H. Evans*. and when his discharge papers came through. moved back to Maine and into partnership with the Lees. All three owned equal shares in the North End Shipyard; all three owned shares of the *Lewis R. French* based on money invested and hours of labor put into her reconstruction. though Foss, as skipper, controlled her fate. The partnership was extended to the proposed new schooner, with the understanding that the Lees would be the controlling owners and at some point would trade their shares in the *French* for Foss's share in the *Heritage*.

   It wasn't a paper partnership. though. with a docile wife thrown in for good measure to give controlling interest to one party. It was a working deal—Linda Lee. like Doug Lee and John Foss. worked as hard and invested as much as anyone else. Decisions were made

Booming up the Penobscot
Bay on a close reach. "I
want a traditional craft,
and that includes the size
of the materials she is built
of, the same size...she
would have been built with
one hundred years ago."

jointly; disputes, the few these friends would have, were settled by majority vote.

A five-year plan for building the *Heritage* was drawn up in the fall of 1978, with the expectation that construction on the schooner would begin in 1979 and she would be launched in the spring of 1984. The intention was to borrow reasonably small amounts of money during the first four years and a large amount during the fifth, when they could expect heavy outfitting expenses. Since they estimated their own labor on the project to be worth $85,000, the total investment would be $315,000. They hoped to get bank loans amounting to $200,000, leaving $115,000 to be raised among themselves. Small loans from private lenders and the summer income of the *Lewis R. French* and the *Isaac H. Evans* would cover that.

As things turned out, the financial estimates were right on the button, but their time schedule was out of whack: They were a year ahead! By the time the *Heritage* was ready for sea in 1983, $300,000 had been spent on the vessel, not including the partners' labor. Almost $200,000 was borrowed from the bank, but not in increasing increments as originally planned. Instead, the partners went right up to the last year on their own resources, then took out a big loan to finish the job. The bank had no quarrel with that: Three years of full-blast building experience was proof enough that they were serious, and a planked-up, decked-over passenger schooner is collateral enough for even the most flint-hearted loan officer.

The market value of the *Heritage*—the amount she would cost if she had been conventionally financed and built in a commercial yard—was well over $500,000. In fact, some people suggest you couldn't build a wooden vessel like the *Heritage* today for less than three quarters of a million dollars.

January 3, 1981
    The past week has been a landmark. The first piece of planking was fastened on. The aft piece of four-inch-thick garboard on the port side, starting at the sternpost and running 26 feet forward. It takes a mighty twist. But after steaming for five hours it twisted easily, and we had plenty of time to work it. The excitement of the moment can really get you caught up. Everyone rushed around pushing and hauling and throwing big clamps around as if they weighed ten pounds, when some of them must have been pushing 80 to 100 pounds. Everyone had sore backs that night....

January 15, 1981
    Six planks today. Most so far....

January 17, 1981
    24 planks this week....

January 20, 1981
    After work today we had a long discussion on the scantling sizes actually required. Haddie Hawkins would build a vessel much lighter. He is correct that you don't need

the strength we're building into the *Heritage*. But what is the real reason for building the vessel?

    (1) I want to be able to sail a large coasting schooner around the coast.

    (2) I want a traditional craft, and that includes the size of the materials she is built of, the same size framing and planking she would have been built with 100 years ago.

    (3) The vessel must last a very long time....

February 16–20, 1981
    34 planks.

March 9–13, 1981
    43 planks.

March 20, 1981
    The hull planking is finished, with the last shutter going in on the port quarter right after lunch. Both happy and sad....

                              —from Captain Douglas Lee's journal

Building a wooden schooner the size of the *Heritage* takes an incredible amount of materials, the cost of which can be secondary to their supply. Think about it: Approximately 100,000 board feet of lumber went into her, three tons of fastenings, two tons of ironwork, a mile of rope, five thousand square feet of canvas, plus all the bits and pieces of working gear—the windlass, galley stove, donkey engine, pumps, steering mechanism, heads, plumbing, electrics—and then the accommodations for thirty-three passengers—blankets, mattresses, pillows, life jackets, eating utensils, pots and pans. Just locating all this stuff and getting it delivered was an exercise in logistics that would deter most people, never mind building it into a ship. It was no mean feat, especially when you consider that most observers believed that some materials, like wood, were in short supply, and others, like ironwork, just couldn't be found.

Three types of wood were used in the vessel: white pine for the decking; red oak for the backbone, framing, and planking; and Douglas fir for the ceiling. The Douglas fir was the easiest to locate: it is in plentiful supply and was custom-ordered from the west coast. Pine and oak were another matter. After all, you can't walk into a lumberyard today and pick out the stock you want in the dimensions required, especially proper crooked stock for the double-sawn frames. The proprietor would scratch his head and ask if knotty-pine paneling would do.

Like the shipbuilders of a century ago, the trio went into the woods for the pine, buying the trees as they stood, having them felled and hauled to a mill, ripping and finish-planing the rough planks in their own shop. They shopped locally for the oak, striking a deal with the Brooks Mill of nearby Thomaston for the best stock that could be found in the appropriate widths and lengths. It was a fortuitous choice, because Karl Brooks turned out to be as interested in seeking out and supplying quality timbers as he was in making money. His perseverance in milling the right stock at the right time for a particular job was part of the reason why the *Heritage* could be launched a year ahead of plan.

What of the impossible-to-find ironwork—the mast bands, the chainplates, the block straps, the yawlboat davits? Finding no supplier for those, Doug Lee decided to make them himself. He set up a forge, read a number of technical books and articles, talked with blacksmiths, and pounded hot steel for a couple of months until the job was done.

It sounds like the philosophy of the logistics branch of the U.S. Army during World War II: If it exists, we'll get it; if it doesn't, we'll make it; if it can't be done, we'll do it.

January 22, 1982

I was fastening the trailboard knees, using the half-inch "hole-hog" drill. I had drilled with one bit and was about to switch to another and was talking to Eric, when I put my left hand on the drill (rushing as usual). The countersink grabbed my cotton glove. My hand went into instant pain. The little finger was torn open and the top joint bent way off to one side. My first thoughts were, Damn, now I won't get this finished today and now I'll be bored to tears waiting for a doctor to take care of it at the hospital, which was true. Turned out it was only dislocated. Never wear cotton gloves while running a drill....

January 29, 1982

Peter is still working on the trailboard knees, Glen finished fairing frames and is now making his first covering board on the quarterdeck. John has four pieces of covering board on the main deck, the other John has three deckhouse grubs all chamfered and sanded, I made the false covering board, which are extensions of the main deck covering boards from the break, aft....

February 15, 1982

The laying of the main deck started today....

March 4, 1982

Today was great. The deck is finished—twelve working days, with four people working. Also the waist and inside rail clamp is finished. Also the watertight bulkheads are splined and screwed on. The railcap stock came from Brooks's, $892 worth. It is beautiful, worth every penny. Six pieces are 27 feet long, the rest are curvy and 16 feet long. All are eighteen inches to twenty inches wide at the butt. We got the deck all cleaned up this afternoon. Looks real impressive....

—from Captain Douglas Lee's journal

Only about six months out of each year were available for work on the *Heritage*—October through March. The other six months belonged to the *Lewis R. French* and the *Isaac H. Evans*. Spring was for fitting-out, summer for sailing, and fall for layup. It was just as well: About the time the Lees and Foss were tired of sailing, it was time to begin work on the *Heritage*, and about the time they were exhausted from horsing big timbers around, it was time to go sailing.

Doug. Linda. and John were the constants during the building of the *Heritage*—on the job every working day. sometimes far into the night. many weekends and holidays—but they were not alone. Word spread quickly along the coast that a big wooden schooner was under construction in Rockland. and willing workers who knew this was a rare chance to practice an ancient trade soon turned up to offer their services. Many were turned away. but just as many were hired according to the needs of the yard and the availability of funds. Some were skilled. some were not. but it was a splendid opportunity to gain experience. since there wasn't much wooden shipbuilding going on elsewhere.

For the most part. Doug and John would work alone or head up a work party. such as the planking gang or the metalworkers. Linda handled the finances and much of the logistics. filling in on the construction crew as required. Even after the Lees' first baby was born in the fall of 1980, and their second in 1983, Linda continued to work full time like the rest of the crew.

The crew ranged from as few as three to as many as ten, with hiring preferences weighted toward those who sailed with the schooner fleet during the summer—under the assumption that such people, even if they lacked shipbuilding experience, could learn fast because they would at least be familiar with the function of the vessel on which they were working. Some of the stalwarts were Captain Ed Glaser (currently the skipper of the *Isaac H. Evans*), Glen Brooks, Erma Colvin, Eric Peterson, and Peter Drury. Part-timers included Haddie Hawkins, formerly of the schooner *Mary Day*, a number of apprentices on loan from the Apprenticeshop of the Maine Maritime Museum in Bath, and various specialists who were hired to do particular jobs.

October 26, 1982
    Linda and Gino caulked the deck this summer. Linda is caulking the topsides now....

November 17, 1982
    The last piece of lead ballast went on today. It took 132 feet of stainless steel rod to hang it on....

November 29, 1982
    John has been framing and putting joinerwork around the pump room and the shower room. Erma and Eric have the forecastle varnished and are now working in the amidships compartment. Glen and I got the donkey engine running on Saturday. I spent some of last week taking the anchor windlass apart so a new, longer shaft can be made....

December 25, 1982
    I've been working away at the forge. Have the power hammer running now, which makes the ironwork move right along. The first thing I made was the end of the jibboom iron out of $1/2$" x 3" stock with $3/4$" ears welded on, filed, and ground down smooth....

January 20, 1983
    Tom just finished making beautiful oak stairs for the galley. Erma "the Varnish Queen" will get five coats of Zip-Guard right on them. Erma hasn't just been varnishing. She made and finished twelve gorgeous stools for the galley....

February 9, 1983
    Finished the ironwork, which means ten weeks more or less for the job, two people (Peter Drury and me) full time....
                                                —from Captain Douglas Lee's journal

They launched the new coasting schooner *Heritage* on a cold, raw day, April 16, 1983. At the top of the tide, Linda Lee broke a bottle of champagne against the vessel's forefoot while a crowd of two to three thousand watched. The launching wasn't quite as extravagant as that of the clipper ship *Red Jacket* alongside the same spot 130 years earlier, and the schooner, though an elegant vessel, wasn't quite as opulent as the clipper, but there was a Scottish bagpipe band, and the *Heritage*, distinctively painted with a red bottom, ivory topsides, and red, white, and black wale stripes, was decked out with flags. Newspaper photographers and television cameramen were on hand. As the vessel floated free of the launching ways and the spectators, charmed by a vision of the past they had thought they would never see, a flight of balloons went up from the afterdeck of a tugboat and the steam whistle at the fish-rendering plant sounded a salute. It was a moment not easily forgotten.

April 16, 1983, Launch Day
   Cold, wet day if I ever saw one. I've never seen so many people here. At high noon the excitement started to take over. Was everything really ready? It took about five minutes for the railway car to lower away for the *Heritage* to float. It seemed like forever, time to think over the building, the people involved, the problems. Then she was afloat. But that's far from the end: we have only eight weeks to finish and rig her, to get her working. It looks like a lot to do, but...no problem.

—from Captain Douglas Lee's journal

"One year of thinking, one year of planning, three years of building."

XII *A Passage in Time*

As the years have passed, I've taken time to look back on my many experiences in those old schooners. They were a school like no other could be. I learned that there were times when one could entirely forget himself and perform deeds that might win a medal in a military service, yet be considered routine in a sailing ship.
—Captain Francis E. Bowker, *Atlantic Four-Master:*
The Story of the Schooner Herbert L. Rawding

Saturday morning, the last of our cruise, came crisp, and the air, in sharp contrast to that of the day before, was as dry as that over the western desert. By seven o'clock, the wind was blowing hard out of the northwest, 15 or 20 knots—gusting at times to 25 or 30. The early morning coffee drinkers were either huddled on deck in the lee of the main cabinhouse or down below next to the galley stove. The temperature was about fifty degrees, but in the wind it felt like thirty-five. The surface of the water in Pulpit Harbor had that hard, purple look common to fall on Penobscot Bay. Out in the bay itself, beyond Pulpit Rock, there were even rows of steep, choppy, whitecapped waves, their leeward sides streaked with lines of foam driven by the wind. Our schooner's standing rigging hummed in the breeze, and the halyards slapped against the masts. The long streamer at the masthead was out straight, as if it had been sized with a heavy dose of starch.

Except for the *Heritage*, a couple of lobsterboats, a cruising yacht, and our schooner, Pulpit Harbor—big enough to hold the New York Yacht Club fleet and then some—was empty. The summer people who lived on this side of North Haven had already hauled their boats for the season, and most of the houses within view of the anchorage were closed down and shuttered up. The only signs of life ashore were a fellow at the head of the harbor bailing a small rowboat and a woman beating a rug on a clothesline next to an old farmhouse, now part of a gentleman's farm, on the point by the harbor entrance.

Over on the *Heritage*, a passenger in swimming trunks climbed up on the port rail, stood there for a few moments contemplating the horizon, and then did a half-gainer into the frigid water. In ten seconds flat (our mate timed it), he was back on deck, wrapped in a towel, shivering. At a distance, we couldn't see whether his lips were blue, but we could well imagine they were. At the warmest of times, the water temperature on the Maine coast might reach the high fifties; on a morning like this, it would be considerably less.

Life slows to a crawl on Penobscot Bay after the first of September. The summer residents go back to their permanent homes, the cruising yachts head to the westward, the

The *J. & E. Riggin* gets underway for Rockland, her homeport.

A PASSAGE IN TIME 191

local yachts are hauled for winter storage, much of the inshore fishing fleet goes into hibernation, and the passenger schooners, one by one, take their last cruise of the season and are laid up. This would be the last week for several of the vessels; it was the penultimate for ours. ("Can't say I'm looking forward to it," the skipper had said last night. "The last of anything, unless you have really hated it all along, is no fun at all.") In another few weeks, the action on the bay would be confined to the ferries, a few big oil barges and tankers, freighters in and out of the marine terminal at Searsport, the occasional fishing boat, duckboats heading out to the ledges and clamboats for the flats, and not much else.

In the old days, things slowed down considerably in the fall but didn't quite die the way they do now. To be sure, the coasting schooners that worked only the summer cargoes—hay, some species of fish, farm produce, ice (which was cut in the winter and stored in insulated icehouses for shipment to the hot South in the spring and summer)—closed down for the winter and were laid up in protected coves and up tidal rivers and alongside wharves, their crews going home to await the coming of spring. But many of the industries served by the coasting schooners operated year round, and even though most of their necessary supplies may have been stockpiled over the summer months and many of their products could wait until spring for shipment to market, they still depended on the coasters, cold weather and winter storms notwithstanding. The lime trade, for example, operated year round, and the kilns that produced the lime had an insatiable need for cordwood, to fuel the fires. If there were no other vessels on Penobscot Bay during any given day in the late fall and winter, there were always the wood-boats.

✦

The production of lime was, for years, one of the largest industries of mid-coast Maine, rivaling shipbuilding and eclipsing granite quarrying. There were hundreds of limestone quarries throughout Thomaston, Camden, Rockport, and Rockland; approximately 25 million tons of the soft rock was quarried in the region over the years. The latter two towns were home to several companies that operated kilns that produced lime by heating limestone to about 1000° F to drive out carbonic acid gas. The resulting white powdery substance, also called quicklime or caustic lime, was used in mortar and cement, and as a flux for melting iron.

In the nineteenth century, lime from mid-coast Maine was considered to be of the highest quality obtainable anywhere in the country. It was generically known as Thomaston lime, though after Shore Village (also called Lermond's Cove and East Thomaston) broke away from Thomaston in midcentury and became Rockland, it was known as Rockland lime, since most of the product was shipped from that town. At the height of the industry, a million and a half casks came out of Rockland each year—more lime than from any other port in the United States.

Before the turn of the century, when other methods were developed for making lime, the kilns were fired by wood—approximately thirty cords for each firing. Since there were

more than a hundred kilns in operation when lime was king, a huge amount of firewood was needed for fuel, virtually all of it transported by water from every section of the Maine coast and even the Canadian maritime provinces. It was terrible for the environment, of course. Woods and forests were decimated to fill the great maw of the kilns; in a matter of decades, the coast and most of the islands were virtually treeless, and the woodcutters had to sling their axes in a wider and wider area. Ultimately, even though an entire segment of the forest-products industry was put out of business, the best thing that happened to the coastal ecology was the introduction of soft coal and, later, oil for the manufacture of lime. If that hadn't happened, and if the demand for Rockland lime hadn't declined, half the state of Maine would have ended up looking like the Dakota Badlands. As it was, it took decades for the forests to come back, especially out on the islands, which had been stripped of their trees as thoroughly as any clear-cut in the Pacific Northwest today.

The demand for firewood up to the turn of the century may have been bad for the forests, but it was good for the coasting schooners. More vessels carried wood to the kilns than carried refined lime to market. Known as kiln-wooders, most of them were coasters that had become so tired out they were good for nothing else. The best of them worked the coast to the east and west of Penobscot Bay, where the water was more open, while the worst of them—and some were in such decrepit shape they could hardly hold together under the immense loads they were required to carry—were confined to the protected parts of the bay. Their decks sometimes awash, the vessels floating more on their cargo than their hulls, they could always be beached in a pinch. (Years later, at the end of the cargo-schooner era, when the lime kilns had long since been shut down, schooners of the living dead that would have been turned into kiln-wooders instead became pulp-wooders, carrying cordwood to the Penobscot River mills that manufactured paper out of pulp. The *Stephen Taber*, before she became a passenger schooner, was a fixture in that business.)

But there was a time when lime production was proceeding at such a frantic pace that there weren't enough tired-out coasters around to serve as kiln-wooders, so schooners were specially built for the trade. Called St. John wood-boats, or Johnny wood-boats, because most were built in New Brunswick near the port of St. John, they were crudely constructed of spruce and other softwoods and had a useful life of ten years or less. They were strange-looking craft, most rigged and fitted out to the barest minimum—no bowsprit, spartan accommodations, little or no paint, patched-together sails—and they were the butt of endless jokes by waterfront wags, according to George Wasson:

Possibly the general stumpy look of these queer craft gave rise to the old and often quoted dialogue, supposed to have been between two skippers: "Where's the other one?" "What other one?" "Why the one they turned to and sawed that one off'n!"....Not a cent was spent for mere looks, so rough and primitive in construction were some of these wood-boats as to be veritable curiosities of shipbuilding. Some enterprising soul once put an extreme specimen on exhibition at a Boston wharf. For ten cents were to be seen crude and even startling makeshifts of every description. It was easy to believe that the unique craft grew very far inland, as a distinctly bucolic touch was given by an anchor which had flukes consisting of ploughshares, fastened on by wire lashings, while the stock was simply a limb of yellow birch to which bark still adhered.

Many kiln-wooders and Johnny wood-boats were privately owned and operated, which meant they tended to keep a rather individualistic schedule, sailing when the skipper felt up to it and not sailing when he didn't, especially during the winter. To ensure a constant supply of cordwood year round, the bigger lime companies employed their own schooners. At the turn of the century, the biggest of them all, the Rockland-Rockport Lime Company, which was formed by the amalgamation of scores of small- and medium-size producers, owned a fleet of about 150 schooners: Half were kiln-wooders and half were lime coasters (or limers), which carried the casks of refined lime to such ports as Portland, Boston, Providence, and New York. Their headquarters, and the site of the kilns that were the center of activity, were within a stone's throw of today's North End Shipyard in Rockland, where our schooner was homeported. The kilns, in ruins, are still there, built into a high bluff at the edge of that section of the harbor. (There are kiln ruins in Rockport, too, at the head of the harbor in that town's Marine Park, as well as several nearby lime heaps and an old steam engine that once was used to haul limestone from the quarries over a narrow-gauge railroad built especially for the trade.)

While the wood-boats were the crudest of the schooner fleet, the limers were of a much higher caliber. A lime schooner had to be tight and strong, since no water could be allowed to come in contact with the lime itself or a conflagration would result. Fire, for obvious reasons, was always feared on wooden vessels. Once it took hold, it was very difficult to put out, no matter the cargo, and it was nearly impossible to quench on limers, because water would fuel the fire rather than choke it. Lime in the presence of water slaked rapidly, producing an incredible amount of heat. As slaking lime also expanded rapidly, wet lime casks could burst, putting even more lime in contact with water, and in turn creating more heat. Unless choked, the resulting fire could spread from the wooden casks to the timbers of the vessel, and then it would be only a matter of time before she had to be abandoned.

The only way to fight a fire on a limer was to stifle the supply of oxygen, a long, drawn-out affair that could put a vessel out of commission for weeks and even months. As soon as the smell of slaking lime was detected, the crew would move all their clothes and provisions out onto the deck, and as the skipper steered the schooner into the nearest cove—the more isolated the better—they would set to work closing up all the deck and hull openings: hatches, scuttles, smokepipes, portholes, anything that admitted air below. They would break open a cask of lime and mix the substance with water to make plaster, which they would use to seal cracks around the openings and in the deck and topside plank seams. Then they would sit back to wait out the fire. Small fires would make the deck hot; worse fires would blister the paint; the worst would break through the planking and eventually burn the vessel to the waterline. For every fire that was smothered, scores were never put out. Scorched bones of burned limers lie on the bottom of many coves and harbors on the Maine coast, especially Rockport and Rockland, whose inhabitants in the old days were used to seeing smoking schooners at anchor on a regular basis.

Even if a lime schooner survived a fire, she was most likely too far gone to reenter the trade. Slaking lime expanded two or three times in volume, and in a tightly packed hold, it put enough pressure on the structure of a hull to buckle the planks and weaken the timbers. No longer suitable for carrying lime, leaking like the proverbial sieve, the survivors were either abandoned as unsafe or introduced to the bottom of the schooner trade; that is, they became kiln-wooders or pulpers or, at best, short-haul lumber coasters.

But that was then and this was now, and the last limer passed this way under sail a long, long time ago. Though there is a huge working limestone quarry in Thomaston, the cement manufactured there goes over the road to market in tractor-trailers, not coasting schooners, and the idea that it ever will do that again hasn't crossed anyone's mind in years and probably never will. The lumber schooners are gone, the pilotboats are gone, the fishing schooners, the bay coasters, the stone droghers, the traders, the Boston coasters, the hay schooners, the three-, four-, five-, six-masters that once represented the epitome of efficient transport of bulk cargoes under sail, anywhere at any time—they are all gone. What is left are a few vessels, mostly in poor condition, serving as museum displays, a few rotting hulks along the shore, and the vessels like ours of the passenger-schooner fleet. If you want to study the days of commercial sail on the coast of Maine, you can read books, examine old photographs, or go to a museum. If you want to experience them, you can spend a week on our schooner or one of the others like it.

You would think that this would be seen as a commendable opportunity, that sailing aboard the *Grace Bailey*, for example—a vessel that has coasted with the best of them for more than a century and still looks substantially the same as she always has—would be seen as the chance to get as close to the real thing as possible in an age that has given us Disney World, Williamsburg, and South of the Border. Yet, strangely enough, there are lots of people—usually those who know little about the glorious past of the coasting fleet and the early years of struggle for the passenger schooners, almost always those who have never sailed on a schooner like ours and would be surprised by the experience if they did—who think that a week on a "dude cruiser" or "skinboat" is something of a cross between a day on the water slide at Wet 'n' Wild and a long holiday weekend on the Love Boat.

Granted, a week on the *Grace Bailey* won't be quite the same as a month trying to smother a fire on a coaster packed from keel to deckbeams with broken casks of slaked quicklime, or a few days next to a coal dock in Portland, down in the hold trimming cargo in the dim light. After all, wearing a lumberjack's red-and-black-checked woolen shirt won't make you a lumberjack. But if your head is screwed on right, if your frame of mind is such that the bay and the sailing vessels on it are viewed with a larger sweep, you will be rewarded with a passage in time that you will never forget.

✵

A cruise on a passenger schooner may be a rough approximation of the old days when cargo moved along the coast under sail, but as the years roll along and we get farther and

"His passengers slept in bunks the same as those of sailors who served on the commercial cargo carriers; they drank water from the same casks, washed their faces and hands in the same tin basins, and read the Sears, Roebuck catalog in the same heads." The *Mercantile*.

operators don't have that luxury. The schooner supply is low and prices are high. Newcomers to the business must invest thousands of dollars to get started—hundreds of thousands if they are considering a new vessel. The fitting-out expenses of the *Heritage*—never mind the cost of building the vessel itself—were $15,000 for the sails; $15,000, masts and spars; $500, life jackets; $1,000, life raft; $1,800, blankets and pillows; $2,500, galley gear; $5,000, navigation equipment; $3,000, running rigging; $5,000, engine for the yawlboat; $2,000, paint. With expenditures like that, meeting the competition takes on new meaning.

Nor is the cost of getting into the business the only element heating up the competition. Approximately two-thirds of the average schooner's gross income goes into operating and maintenance expenses, which get higher every year. Insurance is both expensive and difficult to obtain; few underwriters understand sailing vessels anymore, and most don't want to be bothered with them. Traditional gear and rigging is difficult to find and expensive to purchase. Skilled shipwrights are in short supply, and marine railways equipped to haul and maintain large wooden vessels are becoming increasingly rare. Even berthing space has become a problem—which in many ways says much about the changing nature of the business.

The *Roseway.*

In the early years of the passenger-schooner business, it was relatively easy to find a convenient place to berth a vessel between trips. The owners of docks and wharves that were lying idle, no longer required for loading and unloading bulk cargo, were happy to lease space to a passenger schooner. Camden, until a few years ago the main homeport of the fleet, welcomed the schooners, which used both private and public wharves in the inner harbor. But as Camden made the shift from a local economy founded on manufacturing and shipbuilding to one based on tourism, waterfront property became premium property. Much more money could be made by leasing space to "gifte shoppes," selling waterfront property to condominium developers, and renting wharves and moorings to yachts than could be made from the passenger-schooner fleet. As a result, the majority of the fleet is homeported in Rockland these days, as the harbor is larger, the city itself has yet to see the pressures of waterfront development brought about by tourism, and the city fathers still recognize a good thing when they see it, while those of Camden do not.

Too bad for Camden, which has a maritime tradition going back a couple of hundred years and is in danger of losing it if the rest of her passenger schooners move to other ports. Once one of the major shipbuilding towns of Penobscot Bay, Camden produced hundreds of wooden vessels, including a couple of clippers (the *Benjamin Howard* and the *National Eagle*, later renamed the *Wandering Jew*) and the first six-masted schooner, the *George W. Wells*. Camden's Holly Bean yard alone built more than fifty vessels, including seventeen three-masted schooners, twenty-four four-masters, twelve five-masters, and one six-master. The town even built wooden vessels, among them minesweepers and salvage tugs, during World War II.

But the maritime tradition is just as rich in Rockland, our schooner's home. The crossroads of coastal commerce, it jumped with activity in the old days. The harborfront was crowded with wharves serving the coasting-schooner fleets and the steamboat lines that connected mid-coast Maine with towns and cities to the eastward and westward. The great clippers *Defiance*, *Rattler*, and *Red Jacket* were built in Rockland, as were hundreds of schooners, brigs, barks, brigantines, sloops, tugboats, steamers, barges, and other watercraft of every description. In the 1920s and 1930s, it became the last resting place for many laid-up coasting schooners and was a favored destination of waterfront crawlers looking for decaying evidence of the Great Age of Coastal Sail. Although only the occasional passenger vessel berthed in the harbor before the 1970s, it has now become the principal windjammer port of Maine.

"The sailing weather was so
perfect, so superb, that he
tacked the schooner in the
middle of the bay...and fell
in step with the *Mary Day*
for a brief pickup race."

The *Heritage* was first out of Pulpit Harbor, pushing past with her yawlboat astern as our mate was priming the donkey engine. Fifteen minutes later, we had our anchor up and secured. Then we pushed out ourselves, bucking the strong northwest wind but at least assisted by an ebbing tide. We stayed under power until we were well out into the bay past Pulpit Rock, set all the sails, and squared away on a long board to the southwest that would take us into Rockland Harbor. A few passengers went below to pack their bags, but most stayed on deck to take in the spectacular views. From where we were, we could see the entire sweep of Penobscot Bay: the Camden Hills, the midbay islands of Islesboro and North Haven and the emerging corner of Vinalhaven, the heights of Isle au Haut, the smudge of Matinicus on the southern horizon, the mountains of Mount Desert, the bulk of Cape Rosier up by Castine—all sharply illuminated by early autumn sunlight that streamed through an atmosphere as clear as a crystal glass of spring water.

It was a morning made for photographers, and several on board took the time to record a scene that was now but could have been then, back in the days when the commerce as well as the pleasure of the bay was carried out under sail. Schooners, returning from their week's cruise, were everywhere on West Penobscot Bay, making their way from Gilkey Harbor and the Fox Islands and other eastern points to Camden, Rockport, and Rockland.

The skipper seemed like a man who had died and gone to schooner heaven. "All these boats," he said. "All these types! Could anyone ask for more?"

"Do you go cruising after the season is over?" someone asked him.

The skipper laughed. "Are you kidding? I sail six days a week during the summer, sometimes seven if we take a charter on Sunday, which we've been doing more and more of to keep ahead of expenses. I'm all schoonered out by the end of September, even though I am enjoying every minute of it at the moment. Besides, if you can't tell by now, this part of the country is some cold in the winter. You might find a mussel dragger or a clam digger out here come November or so, but that'll be about it. The rest of us'll be hanging around the house or at the movies or going to that new Chinese restaurant over to the Ames Shopping Center. Hey, Mate! What do they call that new restaurant? China Beach? China Cove? China Harbor? Whatever. It dishes out more MSG than any other restaurant on the coast of Maine."

He said "coast of Maine" as if it were all one word—"coastamain."

"You want to talk hard weather on the coast," the skipper said, warming up to a monologue. "There's a rock on Sheep Island over on the other side of Vinalhaven near Roberts Harbor. They call it Tom Perry's Rock after a fellow who nearly bought the farm back in the mid-1800s. Tom was from Vinalhaven and went duck hunting out on the ledges in late January or February or something like that. He was rowing a peapod. It was a nice sunny day, like today. All of a sudden, the wind shifted and it started to snow and the temperature dropped. Tom broke one oar trying to get back and lost the other overboard. By the time he drifted to Sheep Island—which didn't get its name because it was populated by people, if you get my meaning—it was colder than a well-digger's ass, like twenty below, and darker than the black hole of Calcutta. The only shelter was a big boulder. Tom tucked in behind it and kept himself awake—he was afraid if he fell asleep he'd freeze to death—by chewing tobacco and spitting into his hands and rubbing the juice into his eyes. When that didn't work, he walked around the rock to keep warm. Around and around the rock. Was Tom Perry tough? He walked all night and in the morning took off his red flannel shirt and tied it to the stump of the broken oar and stood there in his union suit in the godawful hellish cold and waved the shirt like a flag to attract attention. Some folks over to Roberts Harbor, probably the Robertses themselves, saw the shirt and went over to get him. They had to cut Tom's frozen boots off his frozen feet, but he lived to be seventy-five and they named the boulder Tom Perry's Rock in his honor.

"You wonder whether they're still tough like that now? About five, ten years back, one of those hard-case clam diggers from over to Waldoboro was crossing the west bay from Rockland to Vinalhaven, right near here, in the middle of winter. He was in an old wooden skiff with an outboard motor. The skiff sprang a wicked leak, a gusher that filled the boat faster than he could bail it out. He managed to get to a big bell buoy before the skiff sank, and he climbed over and tied himself to the bell caging. He was there all night with ice freezing on the buoy. He had a knife and a cigarette lighter and he cut the tops of his boots off and ripped them into strips and made a little tent with his coat. He burned the rubber to keep warm. When a passing fisherman found him the next day—alive, I might add— his face and hands were black from smoke from that burned rubber. Tough? That clam digger was tougher than a boiled owl's butt."

The skipper was eager to get home to see his wife and kids, yet at the same time, paradoxically, he wasn't. The morning was three-quarters gone and the noon hour, docking time, was approaching, but the sailing weather was so perfect, so superb, that he tacked the schooner in the middle of the bay, right by the bell buoy halfway between Stand-In Point on North Haven and the Owls Head Light on the mainland, and sailed back toward Rockport and Camden. We fell in step with the *Mary Day* for a brief pickup race that neither vessel seemed able to win but both skippers engaged in with relish—first the *Mary Day* pulled ahead, then we did, then they did, then we did. Finally, off The Graves, a ledge peppered with shags and gulls and fat seals lying in the warm sun, we turned and ran for home.

✦

Our schooner was the last back to Rockland on that second Saturday of September. If you had been on the Rockland Harbor breakwater that day, you would have seen us coming in, broad-reaching down the western shore with every square inch of canvas set, the American flag snapping at the masthead, a forest-green pennant streaming off to leeward in the stiff breeze. You would have seen us swing wide past the lighthouse at the end of the breakwater, trim the sails, heel with the force of the wind on the taut canvas, and charge up the harbor with white foam in our wake. If your hearing were sharp, you would have heard the thrum of the windward rigging and the shouts of the captain and mate as they prepared us all for one last sailhandling drill. You would have seen us shoot into the wind smartly, drop and furl the sails, lower the yawlboat, push in next to the other schooners moored alongside the old wharf by the North End Shipyard, and tie off our docking lines. If your eyes were sharp and you had a pair of binoculars, you would have seen me shake hands with the skipper and the mate, the cook and the galley hand, cross from our schooner to the *Lewis R. French*, and from her to the *Issac H. Evans*, and from there to the shore. You would have seen me get into my car in the lot behind the wharf and drive up the hill between Jordan's Market and the second-largest dealer in used hubcaps in the state of Maine. In a short while, I, too, would be home.

Bibliography

Albion, Robert G., William A. Baker, Benjamin W. Labaree, and Marion V. Brewington. *New England and the Sea.* Middletown, CT: Wesleyan University Press, 1972.

Aldrich, James M. *Centennial: A Century of Island Newspapers.* Stonington, ME: Penobscot Books, 1985.

Babson, John J. *History of the Town of Gloucester, Cape Ann.* Gloucester, MA. 1860.

Benjamin, S.G.W. "The Weather's Every Caprice." *The Century* magazine, December 1881.

Bowker, Captain Francis E. *Atlantic Four-Master: The Story of the Schooner Herbert L. Rawding.* Mystic, CT: Mystic Seaport Museum, 1986.

Bowker, Francis E. *Blue Water Coaster.* Camden, ME: International Marine Publishing Company, 1972.

Brouwer, Norman J. *International Register of Historic Ships.* Annapolis: Naval Institute Press, 1985.

Bunting, W.H. *Portrait of a Port: Boston, 1852–1914.* Cambridge, MA: The Belknap Press of Harvard University Press, 1971.

Bunting, W.H. *Steamers, Schooners, Cutters & Sloops.* Boston: Houghton Mifflin, 1974.

Carstarphen, Dee. *Windjammer World: A Down East Galley-Eye View.* Camden, ME: Down East Books, 1979.

Chapelle, Howard I. *The American Fishing Schooners.* New York: W.W. Norton, 1973.

Chapelle, Howard I. *American Sailing Craft.* New York: Kennedy Brothers, 1936.

Chapelle, Howard I. *The History of American Sailing Ships.* New York: W.W. Norton, 1935.

Chapelle, Howard I. *The National Watercraft Collection, 2nd ed.* Washington, DC: Smithsonian Institution Press; Camden, ME: International Marine Publishing Company, 1976.

Chapelle, Howard I. *The Search for Speed Under Sail.* New York: W.W. Norton, 1967.

Clifford, Harold B. *Charlie York: Maine Coast Fisherman.* Camden, ME: International Marine Publishing Company, 1974.

Colcord, Lincoln. *Record of Vessels Built on Penobscot River and Bay.* Published in *Sailing Days on the Penobscot,* by George S. Wasson. Salem, MA: Marine Research Society, 1932.

Conrad, Joseph. *The Mirror of the Sea.* London: Methuen & Co., 1935 (first published 1906).

The Crotch Island Quarterly. Stonington, ME: Alternative Energies Project of Planned Total Environment, Spring 1974.

Day, Jane. *Guide to the Maine Windjammers.* Camden, ME: The Owl and the Turtle, n.d.

Day, Jane. "The Return of Working Sail." *WoodenBoat* magazine, November/December 1979.

Dean, Nicholas. "Where Have All the Schooners Gone?" *Down East* magazine, 1981.

de Kerchove, Rene. *International Maritime Dictionary, 2nd ed.* New York: Van Nostrand Reinhold, 1961.

Duncan, Roger F., and John P. Ware. *A Cruising Guide to the New England Coast.* New York: Dodd, Mead, 1983.

Duncan, Roger F. *Eastward: A Maine Cruise in a Friendship Sloop.* Camden, ME: International Marine Publishing Company, 1976.

Frenchman and Blue Hill Bays, Chart no. 13312. Washington, DC: U.S. Department of Commerce, National Oceanographic and Atmospheric Administration, National Ocean Services, 1984.

Garland, Joseph E., with Captain Jim Sharp. *Adventure, Queen of the Windjammers*. Camden, ME: Down East Books, 1985.

Grant, Manley. "Windjammers—Captain Frank Swift's Dream." *Down East* magazine, 1972.

Green, A.J. *Jottings from a Cruise*. Seattle: Kelly Printing Company, 1944.

Keeping the Light: A Handbook for Adaptive Re-Use of Island Lighthouse Stations. Rockland, ME: Island Institute, 1987.

Kemp, Peter, ed. *The Oxford Companion to Ships and the Sea*. London and New York: Oxford University Press, 1976.

Leather, John. *Gaff Rig*. London: Adlard Coles, 1970.

Leavitt, John F. *Wake of the Coasters*. Middletown, CT: Wesleyan University Press; Mystic, CT: The Marine Historical Association, 1970.

MacGregor, David R. *Schooners in Four Centuries*. Annapolis: Naval Institute Press, 1982.

McLane, Charles B. *Islands of the Mid-Maine Coast: Blue Hill and Penobscot Bays*. Woolwich, ME: Kennebec River Press, 1982.

Martin, Kenneth R., and Nathan R. Lipfert. *Lobstering and the Maine Coast*. Bath, ME: Maine Maritime Museum, 1985.

Morgan, Charles S. *New England Coasting Schooners, The American Neptune Pictorial Supplement V*. Salem, MA: American Neptune, 1963.

Morison, Samuel Eliot. *The Maritime History of Massachusetts*. Boston: Houghton Mifflin, 1921.

Morris, E.P. *The Fore-and-Aft Rig in America*. New Haven, CT: Yale University Press, 1927.

Munson, Gorham. *Penobscot: Down East Paradise*. Philadelphia: J.B. Lippincott, 1959.

Paine, Ralph D. *The Old Merchant Marine*. New Haven, CT: Yale University Press, 1919.

Penobscot Bay and Approaches, Chart no. 13302. Washington, DC: U.S. Department of Commerce, National Oceanographic and Atmospheric Administration, National Ocean Services, 1985.

Roberts, Kenneth. *Trending Into Maine*. Boston: Little, Brown, 1938.

Rowe, William Hutchinson. *The Maritime History of Maine*. New York: W.W. Norton, 1948; Gardiner, ME: Harpswell Press, 1989.

Rowland, John T. "Honor Where Due." *Yachting* magazine, March 1927.

Rowland, John T. *Wind and Salt Spray*. New York: W.W. Norton, 1965.

Smith, Edward W., Jr. *Workaday Schooners*. Camden, ME: International Marine, 1975.

Smith, Harry W. *Windjammers of the Maine Coast*. Camden, ME: Down East Books, 1983.

Spectre, Peter H. "The Abandonment of the *John F. Leavitt*." *WoodenBoat* magazine, March/April 1980.

Story, Dana. *Frame-Up! The Story of the People and Shipyards of Essex, Massachusetts*. Barre, MA: Barre Publishers, 1964.

Story, Dana A., and John M. Clayton. *The Building of a Wooden Ship*. Barre, MA: Barre Publishers, 1971.

Tod, Giles M.S. *The Last Sail Down East*. Barre, MA: Barre Publishers, 1965.

United States Coast Pilot, Atlantic Coast, St. Croix River to Cape Cod. Washington, DC: U.S. Department of Commerce, Coast and Geodetic Survey, 1933.

Wasson, George S. *Sailing Days on the Penobscot*. Salem, MA: Marine Research Society, 1932.

The Yachtsman's Annual Guide & Nautical Calendar. Boston: M.J. Kiley, 1893.

Photo sources:

page 36—Bostonian Society, Old State House, neg. 1575

page 43—Society for the Preservation of New England Antiquities, Boston, plate 11695

The *Mary Day.*

Legend

🔆 Lighthouses
--- Route of Our Schooner

Stockton Springs

Sandy Pt

CAPE JELLISON

PENOBSCOT RIVER

Searsport

Belfast

Belfast Bay

Sears Island

Saturday Cove

Northport

ISLESBORO ISLAND

Pripet

Castïne

Bagaduce River

Brooksv

Harborside

CAPE ROSIER

South Brooksvi

Islesboro

Bucks Harbor

Ducktrap

Ducktrap Harbor

Head of the Cape

EGGEMOGGIN

Lincolnville

Lake Megunticook

HILLS

MT MEGUNTICOOK

700 Acre Island

Gilkeys Harbor

Dark Harbor

Great Spruce Head Island

LITTLE DEER ISLE

Pickering Island

CAMDEN

MT BATTIE

BAY

OAK ISLAND PASSAGE

EAST

Union

Eagle Island

Deer Isle

Camden

Camden Harbor

NORTH HAVEN ISLAND

Sunset

Rockport

PENOBSCOT

Pulpit Harbor

N

Rockport Harbor

5th Night

North Haven

Stor

Warren

THOROFARE

North End Shipyard

Stand-In Pt

(FOX ISLANDS)

PENOBSCOT

Thomaston

Rockland

Rockland Harbor

FOX ISLANDS

DEER

Crotc Island

Owls Head

WEST

VINALHAVEN ISLAND

Weskeag River

Cushing

St George River

South Thomaston

Spruce Head

Vinalhaven

Kimba Islar

Friendship

HURRICANE SOUND

BAY

ISLE AU HAUT BAY

St George River

St George

MUSCLE RIDGE CHANNEL

Hurricane Island

Tenants Harbor

Whitehead Island

MUSCLE RIDGE ISLANDS

Carvers Harbor

Brimstone Island

Saddleback Ledge

Isle au Haut Thorofare

Port Clyde

Two Bush Island

TWO BUSH CHANNEL

He

Marshall Pt

↓ MONHEGAN

↓ MATINICUS

Jane Crosen, Mapmaker—©1